It's a favorite American pastime,
and now it's healthy, too!

Grilling and barbecuing your favorite foods
is made easy <u>and</u> healthful with
THE HEALTHY BARBECUING AND
GRILLING RECIPE BOOK

Whether it's for a quick dinner for two
or a crowd-pleasing feast, you can grill meat,
poultry and vegetables without
unnecessary calories . . . this creative
cookbook shows you how.

FAST ◇ EASY ◇ HEALTHY ◇ DELICIOUS

THE HEALTHY BARBECUING AND GRILLING RECIPE BOOK

THE HEALTHY BARBECUING & GRILLING RECIPE BOOK

KARYN WAGNER

Produced by The Philip Lief Group, Inc.

B
BERKLEY BOOKS, NEW YORK

THE HEALTHY BARBECUING AND GRILLING RECIPE BOOK

A Berkley Book / published by arrangement with
The Philip Lief Group, Inc.

PRINTING HISTORY
Berkley edition / June 1994

ISBN: 0-425-14258-2

BERKLEY®
Berkley Books are published by The Berkley Publishing Group,
200 Madison Avenue, New York, New York 10016.
BERKLEY and the "B" design are trademarks belonging
to Berkley Publishing Corporation.

PRINTED IN THE UNITED STATES OF AMERICA

10 9 8 7 6 5 4 3 2

Contents

Introduction

When I was a child living in suburbia in the 1960s, the barbecue was the center of summer family activities. Many homes at the time, ours included, were not air conditioned, so it was a pleasure for my mom to get out of the kitchen whenever possible. Knowing the appeal of building fires, she had little trouble persuading my dad to grill dinner outside. Besides, my mom was a Camp Fire Girl and so my sisters and I became Camp Fire Girls . . . and at a very early age we learned to make a proper campfire and cook in the great outdoors.

Now that I'm an adult, my love of grilling has turned into a career, and I am the owner of two small restaurants in New York City. One of them, Joe's Bar and Grill, specializes in grilled foods. The other, Dew Drop Inn, serves regional roadside and Southern barbecue dishes. Many of my best recipes from these restaurants are included here.

Being at that age where every calorie can spell the difference between fitting into my clothes or fitting into the elevator, I have become very conscious of the type of diet that can promote good health and a reasonable pants size. Grilling foods is one way to provide a well-balanced diet and promote good health. The following recipes are based on principles of nutrition that we now know to be the responsible choice for health and well-being in the 1990s.

Enjoy!

◇ 1 ◇

Getting Started

Grilling is easy and pleasurable when you have the right equipment. There is nothing worse than trying to do a job without the right tools. Here is a rundown of some of the equipment you'll want to have on hand for your grilling experience. These items also make great gifts for the grill chef of your choice!

GRILLS

Hibachi: If you're an apartment dweller, a hibachi is essential equipment for summer in the city. Sold almost everywhere, from drugstores and hardware stores to supermarkets, this inexpensive grill is the ideal purchase for those who grill only occasionally or for that picnic in the park. It's portable, uses only a small amount of charcoal, and is great for grilling up some quick hors d'oeuvre's or a dinner for two or three. The hibachi has one disadvantage: Its small grilling surface makes cooking for a crowd almost impossible.

You can put your hibachi in a well-vented indoor fireplace for use in the house during winter months, but *do not burn charcoal indoors;* it produces carbon monoxide. Instead, use hardwood when grilling in the fireplace.

Kettle Grill with Cover: The most popular grill in every American backyard for the past forty years has been the Weber Kettle grill. The kettle is an oven smoker and grill all in one. It cooks food more quickly and evenly than does an open grill. The bottom vents provide an even air flow, and the entire bottom can be opened for easy ash removal. This grill's 24-inch cooking surface makes cooking for a crowd fast and easy. Weber makes a baby model that is half the size of the traditional model and rivals the hibachi as the city dweller's grill of choice.

Hooded Gas Grill: Easy to light and clean, with no charcoal mess, an outdoor gas grill is a great investment. The heat comes from propane gas, which heats lava rocks or stones, and this serves as a substitute for charcoal. It has two disadvantages, though: You just can't get that same charcoal flavor from a gas grill (though you can add wood chips to remedy this); and this grill produces a fair amount of smoke when fat and juices drip and strike the lava rocks. Still, you can't beat the convenience of a gas grill.

Indoor Cast-Iron Grill: There are several new models of these indoor grills, which you can place on the gas burners of your stove. The cast-iron ridged surface heats up in much the same way as a gas grill. This stove lets you barbecue year round and enjoy the health advantages of grilling—little or no oil, healthy marinades, and little or no salt. Use one of the grills that will cover two burners of your stove, so it can heat up to the proper temperature, and be sure to follow the manufacturer's instructions about preheating it. If you don't allow the grill to heat properly, the food will stick miserably.

COOKING FUELS

Charcoal: Charcoal briquettes are the most popular outdoor cooking fuel. Although starting the fire takes a little practice, once lit, the briquettes burn longer than most other materials. Lump charcoal is all natural, made from hardwood, and comes in several flavors, including mesquite and hickory. It is easy to light and burns at a higher temperature than briquettes. All charcoal must burn down to a gray ash to do the right cooking job. My advice: *Do not* purchase the briquettes with built-in lighter fluid. Oil-impregnated charcoal does not result in wholesome grilled food. Neither does the use of charcoal lighter, which is wholly unnecessary. Be patient and build the right fire for the best-tasting grilled food.

Hardwood: Many grilling purists and campers use wood straight from the great outdoors. After all, why lug around charcoal when nature's first fuel beckons? You can't beat the flavor that a wood fire gives to grilled foods. So when you have the opportunity, gather some firewood and use it in your kettle grill or hibachi. Use smaller wood than you would burn in your fireplace. Twelve-inch lengths of wood about four inches thick work best with a little kindling to start the fire. What's the best wood to use? Hard maple, hickory, or oak. Keep in mind that wood fires are generally hotter than charcoal ones, and it will take a little extra time for the wood to burn down to a white ash suitable for cooking food without burning.

Wood Chips and Herb Branches: If you are using a gas grill, it's a good idea to give your lava stones a little extra flavor boost by adding wood chips. Wood chips, such as mesquite and hickory, are widely available, and herbs such as rosemary branches and fresh thyme can add great herb flavor to grilled fish.

Here are some tips on using wood chips: (1) Wood chips and herbs must first be soaked in water for at least thirty minutes. (2) Drained wood chips can be placed directly on charcoal briquettes but *cannot* go directly onto the lava stones in a gas grill. (3) To make a wood chip "log" for the gas grill, place the drained wood chips on a piece of aluminum foil folded in half to form a 12×6-inch rectangle. Put 2 cups of drained wood chips in the center of the foil and bring the short ends up to make a folded seam. Leave the ends open to allow smoke to escape. Place the open log directly on the lava stones of the grill. Heat the grill according to the manufacturers instructions.

USEFUL ACCESSORIES

Fire Starter Chimney: As I mentioned before, you can't have wholesome grilled food if you use a chemical charcoal lighting fluid. So invest instead in an inexpensive but very effective chimney-style charcoal starter. With only a match and a few pieces of newspaper you'll have a perfect fire every time.

Electric Charcoal Starter: This gadget is great if you have an electrical outlet near the grill. Place the coals over the heating element and follow the manufacturer's instructions.

Aluminum Foil: Aluminum foil is like tissues: you always seem to run out just as you get to the last ear of corn. Buy lots of foil. If you buy it in the largest quantity available you will not only save money but it will be around all the time. If you are near a restaurant supplier or wholesaler, buy foil in the 2,000-foot size. You will be surprised at how inexpensive it is when you buy in bulk.

Spray Bottles: Keep two spray bottles at the grill site. Fill one bottle with water so that you can spray directly into the fire when it flares up.

To be wary of health guidelines, I recommend that you fill the second spray bottle with cooking oil so that you can control the amount of oil you place on your food to prevent it from sticking to the grill. Never spray food with oil while it is on the grill. The oil can flare out of control and cause serious injury.

Skewers: I prefer wooden skewers. They are easy to work with and easy to clean. If you use wooden skewers remember to soak the skewers in water for 30 minutes before using them. I make kebabs so often that I keep the skewers in a jar of water in the refrigerator, ready to go! If you are using metal skewers, I recommend the ones with wooden handles. Even experienced cooks occasionally grab hold of a hot metal skewer and burn themselves.

Long-Handled Basting Brush: This utensil is useful for brushing marinades onto food on the grill. Buy several, as different marinades require different brushes.

Rapid-Response Thermometer: This device helps answer the most difficult question in grilling: Is it done yet?

Carving Board: Buy a wooden carving board with a canal or trough for catching all the great cooking juices.

Insulated Oven Mitts: An essential item! Use mitts to lift the hot grill when moving coals or retrieving that kebab that has slipped.

Spring-Loaded Tongs: Buy two pairs of stainless steel tongs—one pair always seems to be missing when you need it.

Still-Metal Brush: While the grill is still hot, give it a couple of scrapes with a good metal brush. This will keep the grill surface in good order, ready for the next grill day.

Hinged Grilling Baskets: These baskets are available in various sizes and shapes and are ideal for grilling hard-to-turn items like vegetables and fish. Make sure you oil the basket slightly before putting the food inside. This will prevent the food from sticking.

Grill Racks: Enameled racks with small holes are good for grilling vegetables, fish, and anything else that might fall through a normal grill. Place the empty rack directly on the grill surface. Let it heat up, and then brush it lightly with oil so food will not stick.

Fish-Shaped Grilling Basket: For cooking a whole fish such as trout or bass, this is a good investment. It holds the fish firmly in place and makes turning a snap.

STOCKING YOUR KITCHEN

Here are some of the ingredients you'll want to have on hand and some ideas for substitutions when supplies are low.

Oils

Buy oils in quantities you will readily use or store them in the refrigerator to prevent them from turning rancid.

Getting Started

Every oil has a distinctive flavor characteristic of its source. You may use most of these interchangeably, but *be cautious with sesame oil;* it is very distinctive and only a very small amount is required.

olive oil
extra virgin olive oil
hazelnut oil

walnut oil
grapeseed oil
sesame oil

The following oils are light and virtually tasteless. You can use them interchangeably in marinades. You can also brush these oils on food to prevent the food from sticking to the grill.

sunflower oil
vegetable oil
corn oil

peanut oil
soybean oil
cottonseed oil

Acids

As the acidic ingredient in a marinade you can use vinegar, wines, spirits, lemon juice, or other juices.

Vinegar: Vinegar is the product of alcohol or liquids containing sugar converted into acetic acid. The most common vinegars are cider, and white distilled vinegar.

cider vinegar—substitute: any fruit-flavored vinegar such as raspberry or blackberry for an unusual taste
malt vinegar—substitute: beet or nonalcoholic beer mixed with a little white vinegar
rice wine vinegar—substitute: combination of white vinegar and white wine or sake
balsamic vinegar—substitute: sherry vinegar, sherry, port
sherry wine vinegar—substitute: balsamic, sherry, port

white vinegar—substitute: white wine

white wine vinegar—substitute: white wine, vermouth, or champagne

red wine vinegar—substitute: white vinegar mixed with a little red wine

herb vinegar—substitute: white wine vinegar or white vinegar mixed with fresh or dried herbs and allowed to sit overnight

Soy sauce: Soy sauce is not simply a vinegar. It is a mixture made from fermented soybeans, sugar, wheat, salt and malt. Therefore, avoid substituting vinegar for soy sauce. Also, experiment to find the soy you like best; there are a great many varieties. Always use it sparingly!

Spirits: Alcohol finds its way into many marinades and sauces, enhancing the flavors and giving character. Grilling burns off the alcohol and leaves behind the taste. Try adding a tablespoon of rum to your favorite chicken marinade to give your dish a tropical flavor, or add a dash of bourbon to your favorite rib or pork chop recipe.

white wine	Madeira
vermouth	beer
sake	rum
red wine	bourbon
sherry	whiskey
port	

Fruits, Fruit Juices, and Sweeteners: The list of fruit juices is almost endless. Lemon juice and lime juice are the most common and their acidic properties are high, almost "cooking" or pickling the meat or fish with their juice. Use any of these juices for the acidic portion of a marinade.

lemon juice	tangerine juice
lime juice	pineapple juice
grapefruit juice	apple juice
orange juice	guava juice

Sweeteners: Marinades and barbecue sauces are often a sweet-and-sour combination of a sweetener such as honey or molasses and an acid such as vinegar or white wine. Use any of the following sweeteners in your marinades, but be careful when grilling: Sweeteners tend to burn. To avoid this, apply basting sauces during the last few minutes of cooking time.

honey	fruit preserves
corn syrup	molasses
maple syrup	brown sugar

Herbs and Spices

Fresh herbs give the best flavor to simple marinades and to healthy grilled foods.

If you cannot find fresh herbs, use dried ones. Use approximately half the amount indicated for fresh herbs. And to maximize the flavor, rub the herbs between the palms of your hands to release their full potential.

I have grouped the herbs and spices together into types of cuisine. Again, mix and match to create your own unique flavors.

Italian	**French**
oregano	thyme
basil	rosemary
parsley	savory
marjoram	chervil
rosemary	tarragon
bay leaves	

Greek
bay leaves
oregano
mint
cinnamon
cumin
dill

Moroccan
ginger
nutmeg
cinnamon
allspice
cilantro

Asian
ginger
sesame seeds
coriander

Mexican
chili powder
cumin
paprika
cayenne

GRILLING BASICS

How to Lay a Fire

Using a cone-shaped chimney charcoal starter will make starting a good fire a snap.

Fill the cone with charcoal and place a few pieces of newspaper under the bottom grate. Light the newspaper, and it will turn the charcoal red hot in ten to fifteen minutes.

When all the coals are red, lift off the chimney starter and spread out the coals. You should have enough coals to make a bed of 2 inches thick over an area a little larger than the area you will need for the food. The coals should overlap or touch one another.

Or you can use your mom's campfire method: Place a couple of sheets of crumpled newspaper underneath the fire grate of the grill. (I find that newspaper is essential even with a wood fire.) Make sure the draft holes of the grill are open to allow air circulation.

On the fire grate build a tepee of small twigs. Use twigs about the size of fat pencils with a couple of larger ones thrown in for good measure. Heap a couple dozen charcoal briquettes on top of the tepee. Light the newspaper underneath and watch a great fire start.

You can also use the tepee method to start a wood fire. Start the kindling tepee with the newspaper underneath and add larger pieces of wood as soon as the fire can support them.

How to Tell When Your Fire Is Hot

A charcoal fire needs to be gray or white to properly cook foods. When the coals are light and turning gray, spread them about ¼ inch apart. To test for the right temperature hold your hand palm down about 6 inches over the fire. If you can keep your hand in place for four seconds, the fire is medium hot, the temperature I recommend for most grilling. If you want to sear foods, such as a large leg of lamb or a beef brisket, you will want a hotter fire to start. A hand count of two to three seconds means you have a very hot fire, perfect for searing. Move the meat to a cooler portion of the grill to continue cooking, or wait ten minutes or so and continue after the fire has died down.

The adjustable vents in the bottom of the grill will influence the temperature of the coals. Hotter if opened, cooler if closed.

As with most skills, practice makes perfect, and experimentation with your particular grill and the food you like to cook will soon make you an expert. It is helpful to keep a journal of your cooking experiences—for example, fish requires five minutes on each side when using Brand X charcoal.

How to Tell When Meat Is Done

In cooking meat, as in many aspects of grilling, experience is the best teacher. If you want assurance, however, you can avoid the very embarrassing problem of serving undercooked food to seated guests. Test the temperature of the meat using a rapid-response meat thermometer. For beef, lamb, or pork, insert the thermometer directly into the cooking filet. If you want meat rare, it should cook to 140° F.* If you want it medium, it should cook to 160° F. If you want the meat well done, the thermometer should read between 170°–180°. For poultry, insert the thermometer into the thigh section. All domestic poultry should be cooked to 185° F.

*The USDA considers 137° F. the temperature at which the parasite trichinosis is killed. This allows you to cook pork to medium and retain juiciness and be perfectly safe.

◇ 2 ◇

Marinades, Sauces, and Spice Rubs

Grilling food was, of course, humans' first cooking experience, so the technique is not new. What is new is the interest in low-fat foods and cooking techniques, for which the barbecue is ideally suited. Grilling food allows you to use very little oil and no butter. Lean foods such as skinless chicken and turkey benefit from the combinations of marinades and charcoal flavor. Marinades lend flavor to the foods without adding significant calories, and spice rubs are just that—spices and herbs rubbed into the surface of foods to give them lots of taste without added fat or salt. Fish is never better than when cooked over an open fire. Grilled vegetables such as eggplant and zucchini are a boon to the calorie counter, as little oil is absorbed during cooking.

MARINADE INGREDIENTS

Marinades, which are used to flavor foods and tenderize meats before grilling, contain three components: acid, oil, and spices. The types of marinades are endless and are limited only by your own imagination. You'll find some guidelines to basic marinades later in this chapter. Marinades do not add substantial calories to the food being grilled and so are the perfect way to prepare food with flavor but without fat.

Oil: Oil is used in marinades to prevent food from drying out and from sticking to the grill. Feel free to use your favorite vegetable oil in most recipes, but be careful with the stronger-flavored oils such as olive oil and sesame oil. A very small amount of these oils will add a strong flavor to the finished dish.

Buy cold pressed oils if you can. These oils are pressed naturally, and no heat is used in the process—heat releases toxins. They are a little more costly but have a better flavor.

Buy all oils in quantities you will use quickly, or store them in the refrigerator; oils can go rancid in just a few weeks.

Health Tip: You may cut down on the oil in marinades and recipes, but you must use enough to make sure the food does not stick to the grill. To coat the food thinly but completely, put the oil of your choice in a small clean spray bottle and lightly spray the meat, chicken, or fish with a few mists.

Olive oil contains no cholesterol and is very digestible. The American Heart Association states that tests have shown that using olive oil in place of saturated fats reduces blood cholesterol levels. Extra virgin olive oil is from the first pressing of the olives. It is light and tastes very fresh. A few drops of extra virgin olive oil will go a long way in adding flavor to grilled foods.

Other healthy oils for grilling are sesame oil and sunflower oil.

Acid: The purpose of the acidic portion of the marinade is to tenderize the food and at the same time add flavor. Common cider vinegar is used in most tomato-based barbecue sauces, and red wine vinegar is used primarily for marinating meats. White wine vinegar, herb vinegars, and rice wine vinegars will also add distinctive flavors to a marinade. Balsamic vinegar is aged in Modena, Italy, and has a unique taste. Lemon juice and white wine are also common acidic ingredients.

Vinegars are low in calories, and highly seasoned herb vinegars will allow you to completely eliminate salt from recipes. Soy sauce is another common ingredient in marinades as it is also acidic. It is, however, high in sodium. Feel free to substitute low-sodium soy sauce or tamari soy, which is aged and contains much less salt, or dilute the soy sauce with water or lemon juice.

Herbs and spices: Many people these days prefer to eat low-sodium foods. The grilling process is perfect for such a preference because it allows you to cut back on salt without sacrificing flavor. The grilling process itself enhances the food with a smoky flavor. If you want more taste, try adding to your basic grilling ingredients a salt substitute, peppers such as jalapeños or scotch bonnets, and lots of fresh herbs and spices such as cumin, saffron, or coriander.

MARINADES AND SPICE RUBS

As I mentioned before, marinades, and spice rubs add flavor to your favorite foods without adding salt, calories, or fat. Here are some tips to remember when marinating:

Marinades, Sauces, and Spice Rubs

- Always marinate food in a ceramic, glass, or plastic container. Plastic bags that can be completely sealed are great; a gentle shake will turn all the food, ensuring even marinating. Never use a metal bowl or pan. The metal will react with the acid in your marinade and spoil the flavor of the food.
- Fish requires very little time to marinate: 1 hour at room temperature or 3 to 4 hours in the refrigerator.
- Poultry and meats need to marinate for 2 to 3 hours at room temperature or overnight in the refrigerator.
- Always bring food to room temperature before grilling. Fish should stand for 1 hour and poultry or meats for 3 to 4 hours to come to room temperature. You can transport food to a picnic site without refrigeration as long as the food is not in a hot car trunk.
- Because marinades act as a preservative, food can easily be kept in a marinade in the refrigerator for a couple of days. Remember, though, the longer the food marinates, the more highly seasoned it will be.
- Use leftover marinade to baste foods and keep them moist on the grill. Use a long-handled basting brush, and be careful of flare-ups. Marinades containing tomato or honey and other sweeteners such as brown sugar or molasses will brown quickly, so use them for basting toward the end of cooking to avoid blackening.

MARINADES

White Wine Herb Marinade

Makes approx. 1¾ cups

This marinade works particularly well on fish. Use your favorite herbs here. You might consider tarragon, dill, basil, and oregano.

1   cup white wine
    Juice of 1 small lemon
½   cup olive oil
3   tablespoons combined chopped fresh herbs
2   tablespoons parsley, chopped
    Salt and pepper to taste

Combine all ingredients and mix well. Add salt and pepper to taste.

Vermouth and Juniper Berry Marinade

Makes approx. ¾ cup

½ cup dry vermouth
10 juniper berries, lightly crushed (use a heavy can or glass and crush lightly on a cutting board)
¼ cup olive oil
2 tablespoons dried thyme
1 tablespoon dried rosemary
1 teaspoon pepper

Combine all ingredients and mix well.

Basic Marinade for Fish

Makes approx. 1 cup

1 cup olive oil
¼ cup soy sauce
2 tablespoons sesame oil
3 tablespoons fresh ginger, minced
2 tablespoons garlic, minced
¼ cup cilantro, chopped
3 green onions, chopped
3 tablespoons rice wine vinegar

Combine all ingredients and mix well.

Balsamic Marinade

Makes approx. 1 cup

While great for chicken, this is also a perfect and quick marinade for steaks or for sirloin cubes to be threaded on skewers.

¼ cup balsamic vinegar
⅔ cup olive oil
2 tablespoons combined chopped fresh herbs such as parsley, tarragon, oregano, basil or thyme
2 garlic cloves, finely chopped
2 tablespoons Worcestershire sauce

Place the vinegar in a glass bowl and whisk in the oil. When combined, add remaining ingredients and mix well.

Teriyaki Marinade

Makes approx. 1½ cups

This is much better than the bottled version and one less thing to keep stocked in your kitchen. Use it with turkey, chicken, pork, or lamb.

½ **cup soy sauce**
⅓ **cup dry sherry**
¼ **cup brown sugar**
¼ **cup rice wine vinegar**
4 **tablespoons vegetable oil**
2 **garlic cloves, minced**
1 **tablespoon ground ginger**

Combine all ingredients in a glass bowl.

BARBECUE SAUCES

It seems that all cooks have their own special barbecue sauce. Here is a basic recipe followed by a few suggestions for customizing it. You may also take your favorite brand and add these ideas to them.

Basic Barbecue Sauce

Makes approx. 2½ cups

1   **cup onions, finely chopped**
2   **garlic cloves, finely chopped**
¼   **cup (½ stick) butter**
1   **teaspoon paprika**
1   **tablespoon pepper**
2   **tablespoons fresh lemon juice**
1   **teaspoon dry mustard**
½   **teaspoon hot pepper sauce**
½   **teaspoon salt**
¼   **cup cider vinegar**
1   **can (16 oz.) tomato sauce**

Sauté onions and garlic in butter until soft. Add all other ingredients except tomato sauce and cook 5 minutes.

Stir in tomato sauce. Lower heat, and cook 15 minutes.

Tennessee Favorite Barbecue Sauce

Makes approx. 4 1/3 cups

1   quart Basic Barbecue Sauce
1/4 cup bourbon
1   teaspoon dry mustard
2   tablespoons molasses

Combine ingredients and heat up to desired temperature.

Mexican-Style Barbecue Sauce

Makes approx. 4 cups

1   quart Basic Barbecue Sauce
1   tablespoon oil
2   jalapeños, chopped
2   tablespoons cilantro, chopped
2   garlic cloves, chopped
2   tablespoons fresh lemon juice

Sauté the jalapeños and garlic in the oil for 2–3 minutes.
Add the remaining ingredients. Heat to desired temperature.

Island Barbecue Sauce

Makes approx. 4¾ cups

1   quart Basic Barbecue Sauce
2   teaspoons brown sugar
4   tablespoons pineapple juice
4   tablespoons dark rum
¼   cup orange juice
2   tablespoons hot pepper sauce

Whisk together all ingredients in a medium glass bowl.

Hoisin Barbecue Sauce

Makes approx. 1¾ cups

This is a great marinade for shrimp, scallops, chicken, or turkey.

⅓ cup honey
¼ cup soy sauce
 1 large garlic clove, minced
⅓ cup hoisin sauce
½ teaspoon dry mustard
¼ cup white vinegar

Whisk together all ingredients in a medium glass bowl.

SPICE RUBS

Spice rubs are used to flavor foods that require a long cooking time on the grill, such as beef brisket, pork ribs, and chicken parts. The rubs are especially helpful when you're planning to use a tomato-based or honey-based barbecue sauce, which will often burn if used too early in the cooking process.

Spice rubs are like barbecue sauces: every cook has a closely guarded secret recipe. Here are some mixtures to use as a basis for your own customized rub.

Basic Barbecue Dry Rub

Makes approx. 1 cup

2   teaspoons cayenne
2   tablespoons chili powder
2   tablespoons cumin
2   tablespoons dark brown sugar
1   tablespoon dried oregano
4   tablespoons paprika
2   tablespoons salt
1   tablespoon sugar
1   tablespoon white pepper
1   tablespoon black pepper

Mix all ingredients and store in an airtight container.

Dew Drop Inn Spice Rub

Makes approx. 1 cup

2   **tablespoons garlic powder**
2   **tablespoons onion powder**
2   **tablespoons chili powder**
2   **tablespoons paprika**
2   **tablespoons pepper**
2   **tablespoons salt**
1   **tablespoon cayenne**

Mix all ingredients and rub generously over chicken, pork, or skirt steaks.

Indian-Style Tandoori Spice Rub

Makes approx. ⅓ cup

2	**tablespoons curry powder**
1	**tablespoon paprika**
½	**tablespoon cayenne**
1	**tablespoon garlic powder**
1	**tablespoon ground ginger**
½	**teaspoon dry mustard**
1	**teaspoon ground coriander**

Mix all ingredients and rub generously over chicken.

Cajun-Style Spice Rub

Makes approx. 1/4 cup

You'll no longer need to buy expensive commercial Cajun spice. From now on, you can create your own.

1   **tablespoon paprika**
2½ **teaspoons salt**
1   **teaspoon onion powder**
1   **teaspoon garlic powder**
1   **teaspoon cayenne**
¾   **teaspoon white pepper**
¾   **teaspoon black pepper**
½   **teaspoon dried thyme**
½   **teaspoon dried oregano**

Mix all ingredients and store in an airtight container.

Jamaican Jerk Spice Rub

Makes approx. ½ cup

These Jamaican flavors really pack a punch. Use this rub on chicken or pork chops.

1   **red onion, chopped**
¼   **cup green onion tops, coarsely chopped**
3   **teaspoons fresh thyme or 1½ teaspoons dried thyme**
2   **teaspoons salt**
1   **teaspoon ground allspice**
¼   **teaspoon ground nutmeg**
½   **teaspoon ground cinnamon**
5   **small jalapeños**
4   **teaspoons white pepper**

Process all ingredients in a food processor for 15 pulses. Spread the mixture over meat or poultry to cure.

This spice rub will keep for several days in the refrigerator. To keep it longer, cover the mixture with a thin layer of olive oil.

◇ 3 ◇

16 New Variations
on the Burger

Burgers are the backbone of the family outdoor grill experience. These variations on the theme help make an everyday cookout a special occasion. Refer to Chapter 7 for easy and nourishing vegetables to accompany these tantalizing burgers.

SEAFOOD BURGERS

Tuna Burgers with Teriyaki-Mustard Glaze

Serves 6

3   **pounds fresh tuna, chopped to hamburger texture**
1   **tablespoon garlic, chopped**
1   **tablespoon cayenne**
1   **tablespoon Dijon-style mustard**
1   **tablespoon fresh parsley, chopped**
1   **tablespoon cilantro, chopped**
    Salt and pepper to taste
    Olive oil for grilling
2   **tablespoons Dijon-style mustard**
½   **cup teriyaki sauce**
12 **slices of egg bread or 6 soft rolls**

Combine the tuna, garlic, cayenne, mustard, parsley, and cilantro. Season mixture with salt and pepper. Shape into 6 patties. Brush lightly with olive oil. Grill over medium-high heat for 4 minutes on each side or until done to taste. The tuna should be pink inside at 4 minutes on each side.

Combine the mustard and teriyaki sauce, and brush it on both sides of the burgers. Toast and lightly butter the bread or rolls. Place finished tuna burgers on the toast or rolls. Serve.

Salmon Burgers

Serves 4

1 **can (16 oz.) sockeye salmon or ¾ pound fresh
 salmon**
1 **cup white wine or 1 cup clam juice**
1 **egg**
½ **package (10 oz.) frozen corn, defrosted**
1 **tablespoon fresh tarragon, minced**
1 **tablespoon fresh parsley, minced**
¼ **cup bread crumbs**
1 **small onion, finely chopped**
1 **tablespoon butter**
 Salt and pepper to taste
 Olive oil for grilling
4 **onion rolls**

Lightly poach the salmon. To do this, bring the wine or
clam juice to a boil. Place the fish in the boiling liquid. Boil
for another 2 minutes. Turn off heat. Let fish come to room
temperature.

Use a fork to mash the salmon, including the juices or 2
tablespoons poaching liquid.

Mix in the egg, corn, herbs, and bread crumbs. Sauté the
onion in butter until soft and add to salmon mixture. Season
with salt and pepper. Form into 4 hamburger-sized patties.

Brush the patties lightly with olive oil and place them on
a grill over medium to low heat. Cook for 3 minutes on each
side or until heated through. Place salmon burgers, either
hot or cold, on the onion rolls. Prepare mayonnaise spread
and serve.

16 New Variations on the Burger

For the spread:

4   tablespoons mayonnaise
1   tablespoon horseradish
1   tablespoon fresh parsley, minced

Combine ingredients in a small bowl.

TURKEY BURGERS

Ground turkey is now available in most supermarkets and is low in fat and calories. Unfortunately, a plain ground turkey burger doesn't have a lot of taste. Here are four recipes that make turkey burgers tasty!

Turkey Merguez Burgers

Serves 4

Merguez sausage is traditionally made with lamb, but this version with turkey makes a tasty treat. Serve with a healthy Tabbouleh Salad, grilled pita bread and Middle Eastern condiments such as Tahini, sliced cucumbers, black olives and harisa (a Middle Eastern hot pepper sauce).

2	pounds ground turkey
¼	cup bread crumbs
1	egg
1½	tablespoons garlic, minced
2	tablespoons cilantro, chopped
2	tablespoons fresh parsley, chopped
2	tablespoons paprika
1½	teaspoons cumin
1½	teaspoons ground coriander
1¼	teaspoons cinnamon
¾	teaspoon cayenne
1¼	teaspoons salt
½	teaspoon pepper
	Olive oil for grilling
4	rolls

Mix all of the ingredients together, shape the mixture into patties, and brush the burgers lightly with olive oil.

Grill the burgers for 5 minutes on each side over medium high heat. Turkey overcooks easily, so be careful not to cook too long; the burgers should have some spring to them. Meanwhile, prepare the topping. Serve on your favorite rolls.

For the Pickled Ginger Mayonnaise:

4   **tablespoons low-fat mayonnaise**
1   **tablespoon pickled ginger, chopped**

Turkey Burgers with Sesame, Wasabi Mayonnaise and Watercress

Serves 4 or 5

2	green onions, thinly sliced
⅓	cup soy sauce
1	tablespoon sesame oil
1	teaspoon cayenne
2	tablespoons fresh ginger, grated
1½	pounds ground turkey
¼	cup bread crumbs
	Watercress garnish
4	toasted, buttered rolls

Combine the onions, soy sauce, sesame oil, cayenne pepper, and ginger in a small bowl. Mix well.

Mix the turkey and bread crumbs and shape the mixture into 4 or 5 patties. Add 1 tablespoon of the soy mixture to marinate the patties for 5 minutes on each side; do not marinate longer or they will be too strongly flavored.

Grill the patties for 5 minutes on each side over medium to high heat, being careful not to overcook them.

Place burgers on toasted rolls. Prepare wasabi mayonnaise and watercress garnish. Serve.

For the wasabi mayonnaise:

1   tablespoon wasabi powder
½   cup of reduced-calorie mayonnaise

Combine the wasabi powder and the mayonnaise. Blend well and allow the mixture to sit for 10 minutes at room temperature to develop the flavor.

Turkey Burger Deluxe

Serves 4

2　**pounds ground turkey**
　　Chopped zest of 1 medium lemon
¾　**teaspoon sage**
¾　**teaspoon thyme**
¾　**teaspoon poultry seasoning**
¾　**teaspoon pepper**
　　Dash cayenne
6　**dashes hot pepper sauce**
2　**teaspoons fennel seeds, cracked**
1　**teaspoon salt**
1　**egg**
¾　**cup bread crumbs**
　　Olive or safflower oil for grilling
4　**toasted, buttered rolls**

Blend the ingredients together and let the mixture stand for 30 minutes at room temperature to allow the flavors to develop.

Shape the mixture into 4 patties. Lightly brush them with olive or safflower oil.

Cook the burgers on a medium hot grill for 5 minutes on each side. Place them on toasted buns. Serve.

Thai-Style Turkey Burger

Serves 4

- 1 large garlic clove, chopped
- 1 teaspoon fresh ginger, finely chopped
- ⅓ cup cilantro, chopped
- ⅓ cup fresh mint, chopped
- ¼ cup fresh basil, chopped
- 2 tablespoons fresh lime juice
- 2 teaspoons sugar
- 2 teaspoons soy or fish sauce
- 1½ pounds ground turkey
- 3 tablespoons bread crumbs
  Oil for grilling
- ¼ teaspoon cayenne, or to taste
- 4 toasted, buttered rolls

Combine the garlic, ginger, cilantro, mint, basil, lime juice, sugar, and the soy or fish sauce and mix well.

Add the turkey and bread crumbs and mix thoroughly. Shape the mixture into 4 patties. Lightly brush the patties with oil and sprinkle with the cayenne.

Grill the burgers over moderately high heat for 5 minutes on each side. Prepare the rolls. Prepare ginger mayonnaise spread. Serve.

For the spread:

- 4 tablespoons reduced-calorie mayonnaise
- 1 tablespoon pickled ginger, chopped

Combine mayonnaise and ginger. Mix well. Place desired amount on each burger.

VARIETY BURGERS

Grilled Teriyaki Chicken Sandwich

Serves 6

This recipe works equally well with fresh tuna or mako shark sliced into ½-inch-thick steaks.

3 boneless skinless chicken breasts, cut into 6 pieces (approx. 6 oz. each)
Teriyaki Marinade
1 pineapple, cored, peeled, and sliced into rings (canned pineapple may be substituted)
6 toasted steak rolls

Marinate the chicken in the teriyaki mixture for 3 hours at room temperature or overnight in the refrigerator. Bring the chicken to room temperature. Grill the chicken for 5 minutes on each side. At the same time, grill the pineapple rings, brushing them with the marinade. Grill the rings for 1 or 2 minutes until heated throughout.

Toast steak rolls on the grill. Arrange the chicken and the pineapple rings on the bottom half of the rolls. Meanwhile, prepare the spread.

For the spread:

1 cup low-fat mayonnaise
1 can (4 oz.) diced green chilies

Combine ingredients. Spread on top roll. Place top roll on sandwich.

Grilled Eggplant "Sandwich"

Serves 4

These "sandwiches" may be served as an appetizer to a dinner of grilled Italian sausages or as a main dish in a vegetarian dinner. The best way to present them is on a bed of salad greens. They also go well with Black Bean and Corn Salad, or Tabbouleh Salad.

2 large eggplants, cut into 8 slices ¾-inch thick
   Olive oil for grilling
4 tablespoons pesto
2 large tomatoes, cut into 8 slices
1 pound mozzarella cheese, cut into 4 to 6 slices at
   room temperature
4 bottled pepperoncini, tops removed and sliced down
   one side to open pepper into 1 piece (optional)

Brush the eggplant with olive oil and grill the slices over medium heat for 3 minutes on each side or until soft and golden.

Spread half of the eggplant slices with pesto, and top with tomatoes, mozzarella, and peppers. Place the other eggplant slices on top to form the "sandwich." Grill them, covered, for about 3 minutes or until the mozzarella begins to melt.

Serve.

Grilled Tofu Burgers

Serves 6

My vegetarian friends swear by this recipe, which I serve at my burger feasts. It tastes best when served on toasted buns with sprouts and grilled pineapple.

½ cup soy sauce
½ cup dry red wine
½ cup rice vinegar
¼ cup sesame oil
2 tablespoons hot chili oil
¼ cup olive oil
1 tablespoon chopped garlic
2 packages firm tofu cut into 6 slices 1½ inch thick
   Olive oil for grilling

Combine the soy sauce, red wine, vinegar, oils, and garlic. Set aside.

Remove the excess moisture from the tofu by placing the slices on a cookie sheet covered with a layer of paper towels. Place another layer of paper towels on top of the tofu slices, and set a second cookie sheet on the top of the towels. Put a couple heavy canned items on top and let stand for 1 or 2 hours.

Pour the marinade over the tofu in a ceramic dish and let marinate for 24 hours or up to 2 days in the refrigerator.

Grill the tofu slices on a lightly oiled grill for 12 to 15 minutes until lightly browned on all sides. Baste frequently with the marinade.

Serve.

Barbecued Pork Burgers

Serves 4

Choose your favorite barbecue sauce from Chapter 2 and then proceed with this great burger. Beef or turkey can both be substituted for the pork. Serve with coleslaw and your favorite kind of pickle.

1½   pounds ground pork
3   tablespoons bread crumbs
⅓   cup barbecue sauce
      Salt and pepper to taste
      Oil for grilling
4   toasted hamburger buns

Mix the pork, bread crumbs, and barbecue sauce together well and shape into 4 patties. Season the patties with salt and pepper and grill them on an oiled rack over a medium flame for 5 to 6 minutes on each side. Brush the burgers with additional barbecue sauce as they cook.

Serve them on toasted hamburger buns.

BEEF BURGERS

Middle Eastern Hamburger

Serves 6

These burgers are equally as good when made with ground lamb or with a combination of ground lamb and ground beef. A delicious way to serve them is with grilled pita pockets, a garnish of chopped tomatoes, chopped cucumbers, shredded romaine, and Tahini Dressing, or Tabbouleh Salad.

2   **pounds ground beef**
1   **medium onion, grated (about ¾ cup)**
⅓   **cup fresh parsley, chopped**
2   **teaspoons ground cumin**
1   **teaspoon salt**
½   **teaspoon ground pepper**
    Olive oil for cooking burgers

Mix the ground beef and the spices and shape the mixture into 6 patties. Brush the patties lightly with olive oil.

Cook on a medium hot grill for 5 minutes on each side or until done as desired.

Serve with Tahini Dressing.

For the Tahini Dressing:

½ **cup sesame tahini**
½ **cup fresh lemon juice**
2 **garlic cloves, minced**
1 **teaspoon salt**

Whisk all of the ingredients together. Add enough warm water to thin the dressing to the desired consistency.

Dilled Turkish Burgers

Serves 6

Pumpernickel bread and grilled vegetable hummus are a tasty complement to the Dilled Turkish Burger. It also goes well with a salad of cucumbers, yogurt, sliced onions, and chopped dill.

2   **pounds ground beef**
½   **cup onion, grated**
2   **garlic cloves, minced**
¼   **cup fresh dill, chopped**
1   **teaspoon salt**
2   **tablespoons Worcestershire sauce**
1   **teaspoon pepper**

Mix all of the ingredients together. Shape into 6 patties and grill for 4 minutes on each side over medium to high heat until cooked as desired.

Serve.

STUFFED HAMBURGERS

Everyone loves the classic hamburger, but these variations will make your next burger barbecue something special.

Basic Burger

Serves 6

2 **pounds ground beef**
1 **onion, minced**
4 **tablespoon Worcestershire sauce**
   Salt and pepper

Mix the ingredients together and shape into thin patties. Season with salt and pepper.

Mexican Guacamole Burgers

Serves 3

This recipe can add zest to your basic burger. Serve with a Black Bean and Corn Salad, and lots of tortilla chips.

6 Basic Burgers
4 ounces Monterey Jack cheese, shredded
1 mild green chili, seeded and thinly sliced or 1 can (4 oz.) diced green chilies
Guacamole or salsa

Make 6 patties using the Basic Burger preparation.

Mix the cheese and sliced chili together. Spoon 1 tablespoon of the mixture on top of a burger, continuing until 3 burgers are covered. Top with remaining patties and press down gently.

Flavor with guacamole or a good commercial salsa. Serve.

Blue Cheese Burgers

Serves 3

6   **Basic Burgers**
¼   **cup walnuts, chopped**
4   **ounces blue cheese, crumbled**
1   **teaspoon commercial steak sauce**
2   **teaspoons mayonnaise**
6   **teaspoons sour cream or yogurt**
    Salt and pepper

Make 6 patties using the Basic Burger Preparation.

Mix the walnuts and blue cheese and place 1 tablespoon of the mixture on each of the 3 patties. Top with the other 3 patties. Gently press down.

Combine the steak sauce, mayonnaise, sour cream or yogurt, and salt and pepper. Spoon the mixture onto the burgers. Serve.

16 New Variations on the Burger

Swiss and Mushroom Burgers

Serves 3

6 Basic Burgers
2 ounces mushrooms, roughly chopped
4 ounces Gruyere or Swiss cheese, shredded

Cook 6 patties using the Basic Burger preparation.

Mix the mushrooms with the cheese. Place 1 tablespoon each of the mixture on 3 of the patties. Top with the other 3 patties and gently press down, keeping the filling inside.

Meanwhile, prepare the spread.

For the spread:

⅓ cup mayonnaise
1 garlic clove, minced
2 teaspoons fresh tarragon, chopped
1 teaspoon tarragon vinegar
**   Salt and pepper to taste**

Combine the mayonnaise, garlic, tarragon, vinegar, salt, and pepper. Spoon the mixture onto the burgers. Serve.

◇ 4 ◇

Kebabs, A Family Favorite

Kebabs are easy to barbecue and very adaptable. Feel free to substitute chicken for the turkey, beef for the pork or lamb, and chicken for the lamb. Use whatever vegetables you have in the house, and experiment with new root vegetables such as jicama and yucca instead of potatoes.

Tuna Kebabs with
Japanese Mustard (Wasabi Paste)

Serves 4

1¼   cups Basic Marinade for Fish (page 24)
1½   pounds fresh tuna, cut into 24 cubes
 6   large mushrooms, stemmed and quartered
 1   large red bell pepper, trimmed and cut into 1½-
     inch pieces
 1   large red onion, cut into 1½-inch pieces
 1   tablespoon wasabi paste

Marinate tuna in the refrigerator for 2 to 3 hours. Bring to room temperature. Remove the tuna, reserving the marinade. Thread 8 skewers with tuna, mushrooms, red peppers, and red onion, alternating the tuna and vegetables. Make a paste of the wasabi and ½ cup marinade. Grill the tuna kebabs over medium to hot heat for 3 to 4 minutes on each side, brushing the kebabs with the paste. Serve.

Joe's Favorite Swordfish Kebabs

Serves 4

This is very easy. The marinade was my husband's secret until I spied on him one day.

2   **pounds fresh swordfish, cut into 24 pieces**
24 **cherry tomatoes**
2   **yellow bell peppers, cut into 1½-inch pieces**
6   **small zucchini, cut into 1½-inch chunks**
1   **bottle Wishbone Italian dressing**

Alternate swordfish and vegetables on twelve 8-inch wooden skewers. Place the kebabs in a glass dish. Pour the marinade over the kebabs. Marinate for 1 hour. Remove from the dish and cook on a medium to hot grill for 4 to 5 minutes on each side. Serve.

Skewered Creole Shrimp

Serves 4

1	cup vegetable oil
¼	cup Worcestershire sauce
½	cup dry red wine
½	cup dark soy sauce
¼	red wine vinegar
	Juice and zest of 1 lemon
6	garlic cloves, pressed
2	tablespoons dry mustard
½	cup fresh parsley
	Salt, black pepper, white pepper, and cayenne to taste
2	pounds shrimp, peeled and deveined

Mix the vegetable oil, Worcestershire sauce, red wine, soy sauce, vinegar, lemon, garlic, mustard, and parsley. Season with the salt, black pepper, white pepper, and cayenne. Place the shrimp in a glass dish. Pour the mixture over the shrimp.

Marinate for 30 minutes at room temperature or for 3 to 4 hours in the refrigerator.

Thread the ingredients onto 12 wooden skewers, passing the skewer through tail of the shrimp and then through the head region. Cook the shrimp over a medium hot grill for 2 to 3 minutes on each side. Serve.

Garlic Oregano Lamb with
Olive Oregano Relish

Serves 4–5

¼ cup plain low-fat yogurt
2 tablespoons fresh oregano, chopped
2 garlic cloves, minced
2 pounds lean lamb shoulder or leg, cut into 2-inch cubes
12 small onions, peeled, or 2 large onions cut into 2-inch pieces
18 mushroom caps
1 large red bell pepper, cut into 1-inch pieces
1 medium zucchini, cut crosswise into ¼-inch slices
1 large lemon, cut crosswise into 12 slices
¼ cup olive cup
1½ teaspoons salt
1½ teaspoons pepper

Prepare the Olive Oregano Relish. Set aside.

Combine yogurt, oregano, and garlic. Add lamb cubes and refrigerate overnight. Bring to room temperature.

Thread 8 skewers with lamb, onion, mushroom caps, red pepper, zucchini, and lemon slices.

Grill the kebabs. As you are grilling them, brush them with the olive oil and season them with the salt and pepper. Grill the kebabs for 5 to 6 minutes or until done as desired. Serve with the relish.

Kebabs, A Family Favorite

For the Olive Oregano Relish:

1½ tablespoons fresh oregano, basil, or tarragon, chopped
 1 tablespoon fresh lemon juice
 ¾ teaspoon Worcestershire sauce
 1 teaspoon honey
 1 cup kalamata olives or brine-cured black olives, pitted and chopped
 2 garlic cloves, peeled and bruised
 ¼ cup olive oil

Mix all of the ingredients together and refrigerate overnight. Bring to room temperature and discard garlic before serving.

Honey Pork Kebabs

Serves 4

- ¼ **cup bourbon**
- ¼ **cup prepared mustard**
- ¼ **cup honey**
- ½ **teaspoon dried tarragon**
- 3–4 **sweet potatoes, cut into 24 one-inch cubes**
- 1½ **pounds pork tenderloin, cut into 24 one-inch cubes**
- 4 **medium ripe unpeeled peaches, pitted and quartered**
- 8 **yellow onions, each cut into 4 two-inch pieces**
  Olive oil for grilling

Combine the bourbon, mustard, honey, and tarragon in a bowl; stir well and set aside.

Arrange sweet potatoes in a vegetable steamer over boiling water; cover and steam 12 minutes or until crisp-tender.

Thread 3 sweet potato cubes, 3 pork cubes, 2 peach quarters, and 4 onion pieces alternately onto each of eight 10-inch skewers. Brush the kebabs with the honey mixture. Lightly oil the grill rack and set it on the grill over medium hot coals. Place the skewers on the rack and cook them for 5 minutes on each side or until thoroughly heated, basting occasionally with the honey mixture.

Greek-Style Lamb Kebabs

Serves 4

⅓ **cup white grape juice**
¼ **cup fresh Italian parsley, chopped**
¼ **cup fresh lime juice**
1 **teaspoon grated lime zest**
1 **teaspoon chopped fresh rosemary**
1 **garlic clove, minced**
½ **teaspoon cinnamon**
1 **pound lean boneless leg of lamb, trimmed and cut into 24 one-inch cubes**
1 **eggplant (approx. ¾ pound)**
16 **cherry tomatoes**
    Olive oil for grilling
2 **cups hot cooked couscous**

Combine the grape juice, Italian parsley, lime juice and zest, rosemary, garlic, and cinnamon in a large sealable plastic bag. Add the lamb cubes and marinate in the refrigerator 2 hours.

Cut the eggplant lengthwise into quarters. Cut each quarter crosswise into 6 pieces. Place the slices in a vegetable steamer over boiling water. Cover and steam for 5 minutes. Drain and set aside.

Remove the lamb from the bag, reserving the marinade. Thread 3 lamb cubes, 3 eggplant pieces, and 2 cherry tomatoes alternately on each of eight 10-inch skewers.

Lightly brush the kebabs with olive oil and place them on the grill over medium hot coals. Cook them for 6 minutes on each side, basting frequently with the reserved marinade. Serve with Couscous.

Barbecued Turkey Kebabs

Serves 4

2 pounds turkey cutlets
1 can (8 oz.) tomato sauce
3 tablespoons cider vinegar
2 tablespoons molasses
1 tablespoon plus 1 teaspoon
   Worcestershire sauce
½ teaspoon dry mustard
¼ teaspoon salt
⅛ teaspoon celery seeds
⅛ teaspoon onion powder
⅛ teaspoon red pepper
12 small round red potatoes, halved
2 medium yellow squashes, each cut into
   8 pieces
   Vegetable oil for grilling

Cut each turkey cutlet in half lengthwise; remove tendons. Cut each half crosswise into 6 pieces.

Combine the tomato sauce, vinegar, molasses, Worcestershire sauce, mustard, salt, celery seeds, onion powder, and red pepper in a large sealable plastic bag. Add the turkey and marinate it in the refrigerator for 3 hours, turning the bag occasionally.

Arrange the potatoes in a vegetable steamer over boiling water. Cover and steam 15 minutes or until crisp-tender. Drain and let cool.

Remove the turkey from the bag, reserving the marinade. Thread 3 turkey pieces, 2 squash pieces, and 3 potato halves alternately onto each of 8 skewers.

Kebabs, A Family Favorite

Coat the grill rack with vegetable oil and place it on the grill over medium hot coals. Place the kebabs on the rack and cook them for 6 minutes on each side or until turkey is done, basting occasionally with the reserved marinade.

Indian Beef Kebabs with Corn

Serves 4

⅓   cup water
⅓   cup mango chutney
 1   teaspoon cardamom
½   teaspoon ground ginger
½   teaspoon cumin
¼   teaspoon sugar
¼   teaspoon pepper
⅛   teaspoon garlic powder
 1   pound lean boneless sirloin steak
 2   large ears fresh corn, each cut into 1-inch chunks
 2   yellow onions, each cut into quarters
     Olive oil for grilling

Place the water, the chutney, and the seasonings in a blender or food processor; cover and process until smooth. Set aside.

Trim the steak and cut it into 24 cubes. Combine the steak cubes and the chutney mixture in a large sealable plastic bag. Marinate in the refrigerator 2 hours.

Remove the steak from the bag, reserving the marinade. Thread 6 steak cubes, 4 corn chunks, and 2 onion wedges alternately onto 4 skewers.

Brush the kebabs lightly with oil, and oil the grill rack. Place the kebabs on the grill over medium hot coals and cook them, basting with the reserved marinade, for 6 minutes on each side, or until done as desired.

Chinese Pork and Eggplant Kebabs

Serves 4

1 large eggplant, cut in 1½-inch cubes
   Salt
2 tablespoons vegetable oil
1 pound pork tenderloin, cut in 1-inch cubes
2 medium onions, cut in 1-inch pieces
2 teaspoons hoisin sauce
3 tablespoons soy sauce
4 tablespoons rice wine or dry sherry
1 garlic clove, minced
½ cup sesame seeds

Sprinkle the eggplant cubes with salt and leave in a colander to drain for 30 minutes. Rinse well and pat dry. Cook in the oil to soften slightly.

Thread the pork, onion, and eggplant on skewers, alternating the ingredients.

Mix the hoisin sauce, soy sauce, wine, and garlic together. Brush the kebabs with the mixture and place them on a lightly oiled grill. Cook at medium hot heat for 15 to 20 minutes, turning and basting frequently.

During the last 2 minutes of cooking, sprinkle all sides of the kebabs with sesame seeds and continue grilling to brown the seeds. Pour remaining sauce over the kebabs before serving.

Beef Burgundy Kebabs

Serves 6

1   **cup burgundy**
3   **tablespoons vegetable oil**
1   **bay leaf**
1   **garlic clove, peeled**
1   **onion, sliced**
6   **black peppercorns**
1   **sprig fresh thyme**
    Pinch of salt
1½ **pounds sirloin steak, cut in 1-inch cubes**
6   **shallots or button onions, parboiled 3 minutes and peeled**
12 **mushrooms, stemmed**

Combine the burgundy, vegetable oil, bay leaf, garlic, sliced onion, peppercorns, thyme, and salt. Bring the marinade ingredients to a boil. Remove from the heat and allow to cool completely.

When cool, pour the marinade over the meat in a sealable plastic bag. Seal the bag well, and place it in a bowl to catch any drips. Marinate overnight in the refrigerator, turning the bag occasionally.

Thread the meat onto skewers with the onions and mushrooms and grill for 10 minutes over medium hot heat, turning and basting frequently.

Kebabs, A Family Favorite

Meanwhile, prepare the sauce. Serve.

For the sauce:

1 cup plain low-fat yogurt
2 tablespoons chopped fresh mixed herbs, such as parsley, thyme, marjoram, and chervil
1 tablespoon red wine vinegar
   Pinch of sugar
2 teaspoons Dijon-style mustard
   Salt and pepper to taste

Mix the ingredients together well. Serve with the kebabs.

Smoked Sausage and Apple Kebabs with Sweet Mustard Sauce

Serves 6

I am a big fan of smoked sausage. Its one of those staples I always have on hand. Try these kebabs with Grilled Potato Salad (page 144). Turkey sausages are now available and may be used in this recipe.

1   **cup mild commercial mustard**
¼   **cup brown sugar**
¼   **Apple juice**
2   **teaspoons fresh tarragon, chopped**
    Pinch of cayenne
4   **small apples, quartered and cored**
    Lemon juice
2   **rings smoked pork or beef sausages, cut in 1-inch slices**
8   **sage leaves**

Whisk together the mustard, brown sugar, apple juice, tarragon, and cayenne.

Brush the apples with lemon juice.

Thread the apples onto skewers, alternating them with sausage pieces and sage leaves. Brush with the mustard mixture. Grill for 10 minutes, turning frequently and basting with the sauce. Serve any remaining sauce with the kebabs if desired.

Chicken Tikka Kebabs

Serves 6

An excellent way to serve this recipe is on a bed of shredded lettuce, garnished with tomatoes and a couple of lemon wedges, and accompanied by a Tabbouleh Salad.

12   boneless chicken thighs
½   cup plain low-fat yogurt
1   2-inch piece fresh ginger, grated
1   garlic clove, finely minced
1   teaspoon chili powder
½   teaspoon ground coriander
½   teaspoon cumin
¼   teaspoon tumeric
¼   teaspoon paprika
       Juice of one lime
       Salt and pepper to taste

Cut chicken into 1-inch pieces. Mix together the yogurt, ginger, garlic, chili powder, coriander, cumin, tumeric, paprika, and lime juice. Season with salt and pepper. Pour the marinade mixture over the chicken and stir well. Cover and refrigerate for several hours.

Thread the chicken on skewers and grill it for 10 to 15 minutes, turning frequently and basting with the remaining marinade.

Spicy Grilled Chicken, Shrimp, and Pineapple

Serves 6

These are perfect kebabs for a picnic as they are parboiled before being grilled.

¾ cup jalapeño jelly
¼ cup pineapple juice
36 large shrimp, tails intact, shelled and deveined
1½ pounds boneless chicken breast, cut into ¾-inch cubes
1 pineapple, peeled and cut into ¾-inch chunks
   Salt and pepper to taste
   Vegetable oil for grilling

In a small saucepan combine the jalapeño jelly and the pineapple juice. Heat over moderate heat until jelly is melted.

Alternately thread the shrimp, chicken, and pineapple onto 12 wooden skewers. In a deep skillet of boiling water, cook the kebabs in batches for 6 minutes. Drain.

Brush the kebabs with the jalapeño jelly mixture, season them with salt and pepper, and cook them on an oiled rack for 2 minutes on each side until heated through.

◇ 5 ◇

Fish on the Grill,
Fast and Flavorful

Grilled Striped Bass with Orange

Serves 4

> **Juice and zest of 1 orange**
> 2 **garlic cloves, pressed**
> 2 **tablespoons olive oil**
> **Salt and pepper to taste**
> 1 **whole striped bass (approx. 3 lb.)**
> **Orange slices and watercress garnish**

Combine the orange juice and zest with the garlic and oil. Flavor with salt and pepper. Wash and scale fish and make 3 shallow incisions in each side. Place the fish in a glass dish and pour the orange marinade over it. Cover and marinate for 2 to 3 hours in the refrigerator or for 1 hour at room temperature.

Place the fish in an oiled grilling basket. Cook over medium-hot heat for 8 to 10 minutes on each side.

Garnish with orange slices and watercress. Serve.

Rosemary Tuna Steaks

Serves 4

Grilled Potato Wedges and fresh sliced tomatoes with basil, sage, and pepper are a delicious accompaniment to this recipe.

1 **cup dry white wine**
  Juice and zest of 1 lemon
1 **sprig fresh rosemary, chopped, or ¼ teaspoon dried rosemary**
2 **garlic cloves, pressed**
1 **tablespoon Worcestershire sauce**
¼ **cup olive oil**
  Salt and pepper to taste
4 **tuna steaks (approximately 8 ounces each), cut about 1-inch thick**

Combine the wine, lemon juice and zest, rosemary, garlic, Worcestershire sauce, and olive oil. Season with salt and pepper. Place the tuna in a glass dish. Pour the marinade over it. Marinate fish for 1 hour at room temperature or 2 to 3 hours in the refrigerator.

Grill the fish over medium hot heat for 4 minutes on each side for medium doneness. The fish will continue to cook after you take it off the fire, so don't overcook.

Grilled Tuna with Mint, Garlic, and Soy Sauce

Serves 4

4   **tuna steaks (approx. 8 oz. each)**
3   **garlic cloves, pressed**
2   **tablespoons soy sauce**
2   **tablespoons lemon juice**
2   **tablespoons white wine or sake**
4   **sprigs fresh mint, chopped**
    Olive oil for grilling

Place the fish in a glass dish. Combine the garlic, soy sauce, lemon juice, white wine, and mint. Rub the mixture into the fish. Let stand for 1 hour. Grill the fish over medium hot heat for 5 minutes on each side, brushing it lightly with olive oil.

Chili Spiced Tuna with Grilled-Tomato Sauce

Serves 4

6   ripe plum tomatoes
    Olive oil for grilling tomatoes
¼   cup fresh cilantro, chopped
¼   fresh lime juice
3   tablespoons olive oil
    Salt and pepper to taste
1   tablespoon cumin seeds
1   teaspoon coriander seeds
1   teaspoon chili powder
2   tablespoons coarse salt
2   tablespoons brown sugar
1   teaspoon cinnamon
4   tuna steaks (approximately 7 ounces each), cut
    ¾-inch thick
1   tablespoon olive oil for grilling tuna
2   ripe mangoes, peeled and sliced, as a garnish
    Fresh cilantro sprigs as a garnish

Grill the tomatoes, brushed with olive oil, over a very hot grill until charred. Remove and allow to cool. Remove charred skins and mash tomatoes in a bowl with cilantro, lime juice, and olive oil. Add salt and pepper to taste. Set aside.

Toast the cumin and coriander seeds in a small skillet for 2 minutes over medium-low heat, shaking constantly.

Transfer the seeds to a small food processor or coffee mill and process them to a coarse powder. Add the chili powder, salt, brown sugar, and cinnamon. Mix again. Rub tuna steaks with 4 teaspoons of the chili spice mixture, and let them stand while they reach room temperature. (Store the remainder of the chili spice mixture at room temperature in an air-tight container.)

Brush the tuna steaks lightly with olive oil. Grill them over medium-hot heat for 5 minutes on each side.

Spoon out 2 or 3 tablespoons of the Grilled-Tomato Sauce on a serving plate. Top with the tuna steaks. Garnish with mango slices and sprigs of fresh cilantro.

New Mexico Barbecued Catfish

Serves 4

Catfish is now farmed in the Mississippi delta and is available at most fish markets throughout the country. This recipe is a tasty way to try this firm-fleshed and healthy fish. Serve with Grilled Potato Wedges and Grilled Corn on the Cob.

½	red onion, diced
1	garlic clove, minced
2	tablespoons butter
6	plum tomatoes, peeled, seeded, and finely chopped
4	tablespoons ketchup
2	tablespoons Dijon-style mustard
2	tablespoons brown sugar
1	tablespoon honey
1	tablespoon cayenne
2	tablespoons chili powder
1	tablespoon paprika
2	tablespoons Worcestershire sauce
4	catfish fillets (approx. 8 oz. each)

Sauté the onion and garlic in the butter until soft, about 10 minutes. Add the tomatoes, ketchup, mustard, brown sugar, honey, cayenne, chili powder, paprika, and Worcestershire sauce. Simmer over low heat for 10 minutes.

Brush the catfish lightly with the sauce and place the fillets in an oiled hinged basket or lay them carefully on an oiled grill rack over medium coals. Brush them with the sauce often and grill them for 3 to 4 minutes on each side.

Grilled Cajun Catfish

Serves 6

Using a spice rub on fish is a great way to reduce the calories. For variety, try any of the spice rubs in Chapter 2. You may also substitute red snapper, grouper, bluefish, or trout for the catfish.

6   catfish fillets (approx. 8 oz. each)
3   tablespoons Cajun-Style Spice Rub (p. 35)
    Olive oil for grilling

Wash the catfish fillets and pat them dry. Spread the spice rub over both sides of fish and rub it in.

Let the fillets stand at room temperature for 30 minutes or refrigerate them for 3 hours. Bring the fillets to room temperature. Brush them lightly with olive oil and place them in a well-oiled grilling basket or lay them carefully on an oiled grill rack.

Grill the fish for 4 minutes on each side over medium-hot heat.

Deviled Catfish Fillets

Serves 4

¼ **cup grainy mustard**
2 **teaspoons extra virgin olive oil**
¼ **cup chopped fresh basil**
½ **teaspoon black pepper**
¼ **teaspoon cayenne**
4 **catfish fillets (approx. 8 oz. each)**
    Vegetable oil for grilling

Combine mustard, olive oil, basil, black pepper, and cayenne. Spread the mixture over the catfish fillets and let them stand at room temperature for 1 hour or in the refrigerator for 3 to 4 hours. Place the fish in an oiled hinged basket or grill rack, and grill the fillets over medium high heat for 4 to 5 minutes on each side.

Grilled Salmon with Herb Sesame Oil

Serves 6

1	**cup rice wine vinegar**
¼	**cup soy sauce**
1½	**tablespoons thyme, tarragon, or basil, chopped**
1	**teaspoon sesame oil**
1	**teaspoon olive oil**
6	**salmon fillets (6–8 oz. each)**

Combine the vinegar, soy sauce, herbs, sesame oil, and olive oil. Pour the marinade mixture into a glass dish. Marinate the salmon in the mixture for 1 hour at room temperature or for 3 to 4 hours in the refrigerator.

Grill the fish over medium hot heat for 4 minutes on each side.

Grilled Lemon Shrimp Salad

Serves 6

2½ **pounds medium-sized shrimp, peeled, and deveined**

Marinade
Juice and zest of 1 lemon
½ **cup chopped fresh rosemary**
2 **tablespoons olive oil**

Salad
½ **cup fresh lemon juice**
½ **teaspoon minced garlic**
½ **teaspoon hot pepper sauce, or to taste**
¼ **teaspoon kosher salt**
¼ **cup chopped Italian parsley**
¾ **cup extra virgin olive oil**
2 **stalks celery, chopped**
¾ **cup chopped fresh fennel**
1 **pound new potatoes, slices and boiled until tender**

Bed of greens

Combine the lemon, rosemary, and olive oil. Marinate the shrimp for 1 hour at room temperature.

While the shrimp are marinating, prepare the salad: Whisk together lemon juice, garlic, hot pepper sauce, salt, and parsley. Slowly add the virgin olive oil while whisking to form vinaigrette. Add chopped celery and fennel. Pour over cooked potatoes.

Grill the shrimp over medium-hot heat for 3 minutes each side. Add carefully to salad and toss gently. Serve warm over a bed of greens.

Grilled Scallops with Quick Curried Tomato Sauce

Serves 4

This sauce goes together very quickly on top of the stove. If you want, you may grill the tomatoes for a smoky flavor.

- **2**   **large shallots, sliced thin**
- **2**   **tablespoons butter**
- **1**   **teaspoon mustard seeds**
- **1½**   **teaspoons curry powder**
- **½**   **teaspoon sugar**
- **6**   **plum tomatoes, chopped, seeded, and drained**
- **2**   **teaspoons balsamic vinegar**
-   **Vegetable oil for brushing the scallops**
- **¾**   **pound sea scallops**

Sauté the shallots in butter until soft. Add the mustard seed and curry powder and sauté for 1 minute at high heat to release the flavors. Add the sugar, tomatoes, and balsamic vinegar. Simmer for 4 minutes. The sauce will be chunky.

Place the sea scallops in an oiled fish basket or thread them on double skewers. Lightly brush the scallops with vegetable oil and grill them for 3 to 4 minutes on each side over medium hot heat.

Spoon some of the sauce on the bottom of each serving plate and place some scallops on top.

Serve these scallops with a tossed salad of Romaine, feta cheese, and black olives.

Thai-Style Bluefish Fillets

Serves 4

¼ **cup soy sauce**
2   **tablespoons olive oil**
½   **jalapeño, chopped**
1   **teaspoon white pepper**
    Zest of 1 small lemon
2   **garlic cloves, pressed**
¼   **cup Asian fish sauce**
1   **bunch scallions, green onions, tops only,
    cut in ½-inch pieces**
6   **basil leaves, chopped**
4   **bluefish fillets (approx. 8 oz. each)**
    Olive oil for grilling

Combine the soy sauce, olive oil, jalapeños, white pepper, lemon zest, garlic, fish sauce, scallions, and basil in a shallow glass dish. Add the bluefish fillets and marinate them for 1 hour at room temperature or for 3 to 4 hours in the refrigerator. Drain them and brush them lightly with olive oil.

Grill them for 4 minutes on each side over medium high heat.

Scandinavian Grilled Salmon

Serves 4

½   **cup vodka**
¼   **cup fresh grapefruit juice**
4   **tablespoons Rose's lime juice**
¼   **cup chopped fresh dill**
2   **teaspoons coarse-grained mustard**
4   **salmon fillets (approx. 8 oz. each)**
     Olive oil for grilling

Combine the vodka, grapefruit juice, lime juice, dill, and mustard in a shallow glass dish. Add the salmon fillets and marinate them for 1 hour at room temperature or for 3 to 4 hours in the refrigerator. Brush them lightly with olive oil. Grill the fillets for 4 minutes on each side over medium high heat.

Swordfish Steaks with Herbs

Serves 4

- ¼ cup chopped cilantro
- ¼ cup fresh parsley, chopped
- 1 garlic clove, chopped
- 1½ teaspoons paprika
- ½ teaspoon ground coriander
- ¼ teaspoon ground cumin
  Pinch of cayenne
- 2 tablespoons fresh lime or lemon juice
- 3 tablespoons olive oil
- 4 swordfish steaks (approx. 8 oz. each)

Combine the cilantro, parsley, garlic, paprika, coriander, cumin, and cayenne in a small food processor. Slowly add the lime juice and olive oil in a stream to form a paste. Rub the swordfish with the herb paste and allow it to stand for 30 minutes at room temperature or for 2 to 3 hours in the refrigerator. Allow the fish to come to room temperature and grill it over medium high heat for 4 to 5 minutes on each side.

Grilled Citrus and Ginger Swordfish

Serves 4

My new favorite ingredient is zest of orange and other citrus fruits. Buy a good zester and go to town. Be careful not to go too deep into the fruit; the white pith is very bitter. Use the remaining fruit for juice.

⅔	cup soy sauce
¼	cup dry sherry
¼	cup orange juice
1	garlic clove, minced
1½	teaspoons fresh ginger, minced
2	green onions, finely chopped
1	teaspoon lemon zest
1	teaspoon orange zest
1	teaspoon lime zest
2	tablespoons olive oil
4	swordfish steaks (approx. 8 oz. each)

Combine the soy sauce, sherry, orange juice, garlic, ginger, onion, lemon, orange, and lime zest, and olive oil in a shallow glass dish. Add the swordfish steaks and marinate them for 1 hour at room temperature for 3 to 4 hours in the refrigerator. Bring them to room temperature and grill them over medium hot coals for 4 to 5 minutes on each side.

Tuna Marinated with Lime and Spicy Peppers

Serves 4

A delightful way to serve this recipe is with a garnish of grilled sweet red peppers and a fresh fruit salad dusted with black pepper and balsamic vinegar. Also, take caution. The lime "cooks" the fish in this recipe, so be careful to marinate for only 30 minutes.

4   tuna fillets (8 oz. each)
    Juice of 4 limes (8 tablespoons juice)
2   pickled jalapeños, chopped
2   tablespoons olive oil

Place the tuna fillets in a shallow glass dish and pour the lime juice over them. Add the peppers and sprinkle with the oil. Turn the fish after 15 minutes. Grill the fish over medium high heat for 4 to 5 minutes on each side.

Rum-Soaked Kingfish Fillets

Serves 4

Serve this entrée with slices of mango dusted with pepper and splashed with balsamic vinegar. Also, if kingfish is not available, feel free to substitute red snapper or grouper.

	Juice of 4 limes
1½	cups pineapple juice
½	cup rum
2	tablespoons fresh cilantro, minced
1	teaspoon garlic, chopped
4	kingfish fillets (approx. 8 oz. each)
	Olive oil for grilling

Combine the lime juice, pineapple juice, rum, cilantro, and garlic in a shallow glass dish. Add the fish fillets and marinate them for 2 hours in refrigerator. Bring them to room temperature and brush them lightly with olive oil. Grill the fish over medium hot heat for 3 to 4 minutes on each side.

Grilled Fish and Chips

Serves 6

Traditional English fish and chips are deep-fried and served with tartar sauce and malt vinegar. In our version we have added the malt vinegar to the marinade and eliminated the calories that result from deep-frying. You can serve the fish with a low-fat version of tartar sauce made of ½ cup plain low-fat yogurt combined with ¼ cup fresh chopped dill and a dash of lemon juice.

¼   cup malt vinegar or dark beer
1   tablespoon Dijon-style mustard
1   teaspoon Worcestershire sauce
1   teaspoon dried thyme
3   tablespoons olive oil or vegetable oil
1   pound scrod, cut into 6 pieces
12   medium shrimp
12   sea scallops
3   large baking potatoes cut into 6 wedges each
    Olive oil for grilling

Combine the vinegar or beer, mustard, Worcestershire sauce, thyme, and oil in a shallow glass dish. Add the scrod, scallops, and shrimp. Marinate the fish for 1 hour at room temperature or for 3 to 4 hours in the refrigerator.

Brush the potato wedges with olive oil and place them on the grill. Cook them over medium-high heat for 15 minutes on each side or, if you cover the grill, approximately 10 minutes on each side.

Bring the fish to room temperature and place in an oiled hinged basket or thread it on skewers. Grill the fish over medium high heat for 3 to 4 minutes on each side.

◇ 6 ◇

Poultry and Meat

Lamb Chops with Cumin, Cinnamon and Orange

Serves 4

½   **tablespoon cumin**
¼   **teaspoon cinnamon**
3   **garlic cloves, crushed**
¼   **cup fresh orange juice**
2   **tablespoons safflower oil**
8   **loin lamb chops**

Combine the cumin, cinnamon, garlic, orange juice, and oil. Place the chops in a shallow glass dish. Pour the mixture over the meat. Marinate for 2 hours or overnight in the refrigerator. Bring the chops to room temperature and grill them over medium high heat for 5 minutes on each side.

Grilled Steaks with Secret Sauce and Tomato Salad

Serves 4

One of the simplest and tastiest steaks I've ever eaten. No one can ever figure out what the secret sauce is . . . and it's perfect with the tomato topping. Serve these steaks with Grilled Potato Wedges and Corn on the Cob.

4   rib eye steaks (10–12 oz. each)
**   Salt and pepper to taste**
**   Olive oil for grilling**
4   tablespoons oyster sauce

Season the steaks with salt and pepper. Brush them lightly with olive oil, and grill them over medium high heat for 4 minutes on each side or until done as desired.

Brush the steaks with oyster sauce. Meanwhile prepare the Tomato Salad.

For the Tomato Salad:

4   plum tomatoes, sliced
2   tablespoons balsamic vinegar
2   tablespoons fresh basil, chopped

Toss together tomatoes, vinegar, and basil. Place salad on top of finished steaks. Serve.

Brett's Marinated Loin of Pork

Serves 4–6

My friend Brett loaned me her house and her grill to test these recipes. This is her favorite pork recipe she shares with friends. Serve it with Black Bean and Corn Salad.

4	tablespoons Dijon-style mustard
3	tablespoons honey
3	tablespoons olive oil
3	tablespoons balsamic vinegar
1	tablespoon pepper
1	tablespoon cinnamon
1	tablespoon cardamom
1	tablespoon ground ginger
	Fresh rosemary sprigs
2½–3	pounds trimmed pork loin

Combine the mustard, honey, olive oil, vinegar, pepper, cinnamon, cardamom, ginger, and rosemary in a zip-top bag. Add the pork. Mix well. Refrigerate for 2 to 3 days, turning now and then.

When ready to grill, take some of the soaked rosemary sprigs out of the marinade and place them on the hot coals. Wipe the excess marinade off the pork. Grill the meat, covered, with some ventilation, for 15 to 20 minutes on each side. Let rest. Slice before serving.

Ernesto's Butterflied Leg of Lamb

Serves 6–8

Ernest helped test many of these recipes. This is his family's favorite marinade for grilled leg of lamb. Ask your butcher for boned, untied, and butterflied leg of lamb. You could also use this recipe for lamb chops.

1½	teaspoon cumin
1	teaspoon turmeric
½	teaspoon allspice
2	tablespoons pepper
1	cup olive oil
½	cup soy sauce
¾	cup red wine
6	garlic cloves, chopped
1½	tablespoons fresh rosemary, chopped
1	tablespoon fresh thyme, chopped
	Juice of 2 lemons
	Zest of 1 lemon
2	tablespoons juniper berries, crushed
4	tablespoons honey
1	leg of lamb (4 to 5 lb.), boned, untied, and butterflied
½	cup Dijon-style mustard

Combine the cumin, turmeric, allspice, and pepper in a small, dry skillet and heat until aromatic. In a small saucepan, combine these spices with the olive oil, soy sauce, red wine, garlic, rosemary, thyme, lemon juice and zest, juniper berries, and honey. Heat the mixture until the honey liquefies. Stir until well blended.

Place the lamb in a glass dish and pour the marinade over it. Marinate in the refrigerator for 2 to 3 days. Bring to room temperature; this will take 1 to 2 hours. Coat the lamb with the Dijon-style mustard and grill it over medium high heat for 20 minutes on each side. Cover the grill for the last 15 minutes to ensure an internal temperature of 145°F. for medium rare. Allow the meat to stand for 5 minutes before carving.

Grilled Lamb Shoulder Steaks with Hoisin Barbecue Sauce

Serves 4

Lamb shoulder steaks are much less expensive than lamb chops and just as tasty. Lamb should be served medium rare, so be careful not to overcook it. You'll find hoisin sauce in the Chinese section of your supermarket.

⅓   **cup honey**
¼   **cup soy sauce**
 1   **large garlic clove, minced**
⅓   **cup hoisin sauce**
½   **teaspoon dry mustard**
¼   **cup white vinegar**
 4   **shoulder lamb shoulder steaks (8–10 oz. each)**

Combine the honey, soy sauce, garlic, hoisin sauce, mustard, and vinegar. Place the lamb in a shallow glass dish. Add the honey mixture, and marinate the meat for 2 hours or overnight, turning once or twice.

Bring the lamb to room temperature and grill it over medium high heat for 5 to 6 minutes on each side.

Drunken Pork Chops

Serves 6

Serve these chops with Grilled Potato Wedges.

- **2 cups dry red wine**
- **5 bay leaves**
- **2 tablespoons fresh rosemary, minced**
- **1½ teaspoons ground coriander**
- **½ teaspoon nutmeg**
- **½ teaspoon ground cloves**
- **6 loin pork chops, about 1½ inches thick**
  Salt and pepper to taste
  Olive oil for grilling

Combine the red wine, bay leaves, rosemary, coriander, nutmeg, and cloves in a glass dish. Trim the chops and place them in the marinade mixture. Marinate them overnight in the refrigerator, turning occasionally.

Drain the chops and pat them dry. Season them with salt and pepper and lightly brush them with olive oil. Grill the chops over medium high heat for 6 to 7 minutes on each side.

Pork Loin with Tangerine

Serves 6–8

1   pork loin (4 to 5 lb.), boned, rolled, and tied
12 garlic cloves, peeled and cut into large slivers
1   teaspoon salt
    Juice and zest of 1 tangerine (about ½ cup)
1   tablespoon fresh thyme, chopped or 1 teaspoon
    dried thyme
1   tablespoon fresh oregano, chopped or 1 teaspoon
    dried oregano
3   tablespoons soy sauce
¼   cup peanut oil
1   tablespoon gin
1   tablespoon brown sugar
1   tablespoon Worcestershire sauce
1   cup tangerine juice
2   bay leaves

Make slits in the pork roast and insert the garlic slivers.
Rub salt onto the meat. Combine the tangerine juice and zest
with the thyme and oregano, and rub the mixture all over the
roast.

Combine the soy sauce, oil, gin, brown sugar, Worcestershire sauce, tangerine juice, and bay leaves. Place the
pork in a glass dish. Pour the marinade over the meat and
refrigerate overnight.

Bring the pork to room temperature and grill it over
medium high heat for 15 to 20 minutes on each side,
covered and basting frequently. Let it rest for 5 minutes
before carving.

Sweet and Sour Ribs

Serves 4

I prefer the parboiling technique for cooking the ribs. They always come out moist and are never overcooked and blackened.

3 **pounds country-style pork spareribs, cut into serving pieces**
½ **cup orange marmalade**
½ **cup sherry**
⅓ **cup soy sauce**
¼ **cup dark brown sugar**
1 **piece fresh ginger root 1 inch long, grated**
2 **garlic cloves, pressed**
1 **small onion, minced**
1 **teaspoon ground coriander**

Plunge the ribs into a pot of boiling water and cook them for 15 minutes. Drain them and place them in a shallow glass dish.

To prepare the marinade, heat the marmalade until it liquefies. Add the sherry, soy sauce, sugar, ginger, garlic, onion, and coriander. Stir well. Pour the mixture over the ribs and marinate them for 2 hours at room temperature or overnight in the refrigerator.

Bring the ribs to room temperature. Grill them over medium high heat for 8 to 10 minutes on each side, brushing frequently with the marinade and turning often.

Grilled Steaks with Cognac and Black Pepper

Serves 4

½   **cup cognac or brandy**
4   **beef tenderloin or rib eye steaks (approx. 8 oz. each)**
2   **tablespoons black peppercorns**
4   **tablespoons olive oil**

Place the cognac or brandy in a shallow glass dish. Add the steaks and marinate them for 5 minutes on each side. Wrap the peppercorns in a clean dish towel and crack them with a heavy saucepan or a heavy can. Pat the steaks dry with a paper towel and press each steak into the peppercorns. Brush the steaks lightly with olive oil and grill them over moderate high heat for 4 to 5 minutes on each side for medium or until meat is cooked as desired.

Grilled Beef Tenderloin with Balsamic Vinegar

Serves 4

Serve these beef filets with Grilled Potato Wedges.

¼ **cup olive oil**
1 **cup balsamic vinegar**
4 **fresh rosemary sprigs, chopped**
8 **beef tenderloin filets (approx. 4 oz. each)**
   Salt and pepper to taste

Combine the oil and vinegar with the rosemary. Add the beef tenderloins and marinate them at room temperature for 5 minutes on each side. Season the filets with salt and pepper and grill them for 4 minutes each side, or until cooked as desired.

Beef Satay with Peanut Sauce

Serves 4 as an appetizer

These snacks from Indonesia are a favorite grilled appetizer. Serve the satay before dinner with cocktails while waiting for the main course to cook. You can also make these with chicken or turkey.

It is helpful to freeze the meat for 15 minutes before preparing satay; this makes it easier to cut the strips.

½	**pound boneless sirloin**
3	**tablespoons orange juice**
1½	**teaspoons molasses**
1	**teaspoon oil**
1	**teaspoon soy sauce**
1	**garlic clove, crushed**
3	**small slices ginger, crushed**
¼	**teaspoon salt**
⅛	**teaspoon pepper**

Cut the beef against the grain into 2-inch-wide strips. Combine the orange juice, molasses, oil, soy sauce, garlic, ginger, salt, and pepper in a shallow glass dish. Marinate the beef in the mixture overnight.

Bring the beef to room temperature and thread the strips onto water-soaked wooden skewers, leaving 2 inches free at the end of each skewer. Grill the beef for 2 to 3 minutes on each side. Meanwhile, prepare the Peanut Sauce.

For the peanut sauce:

½   **cup smooth peanut butter**
1   **tablespoon lemon or lime juice**
1   **teaspoon soy sauce**
1   **tablespoon brown sugar**
1   **tablespoon peanut oil**
1   **tablespoon shallot or onion, minced**
½   **teaspoons garlic, minced**
½   **teaspoon ground coriander**
¼   **teaspoon red pepper flakes**
½   **cup water**

Combine ingredients in a small food processor or blender. Process until smooth. The mixture should have the consistency of thick soup. If the mixture seems too thick, stir in a little warm water. Serve the sauce as a dip with the prepared Beef Satay.

Grilled Margarita Chicken with Salsa

Serves 4

A favorite at the Dew Drop Inn, this is a quick and easy marinade. Garnish the chicken with lime wedges and serve it with a good-quality commercial salsa and our Black Bean and Corn Salad (page 148).

½ **cup tequila**
¼ **cup lime juice**
½ **cup orange juice or triple sec**
½ **teaspoon red pepper flakes**
 4 **boneless chicken breasts**

Combine the tequila, lime juice, orange juice or triple sec, and pepper in a shallow glass dish. Add the chicken and marinate it overnight in the refrigerator.

Bring the chicken to room temperature and grill it over medium high heat for 4 to 5 minutes on each side.

Garlic-Herb Chicken

Serves 4

4 garlic cloves, peeled
1 piece ginger (approx. 2 in. long), peeled and sliced thin
2 teaspoons paprika
½ teaspoon cayenne
⅓ cup fresh lemon juice
1 cup mild olive oil
2 bunches cilantro, chopped (approx. ⅓ cup)
6 green onions, chopped (approx. ⅓ cup)
Pepper to taste
2 chickens, halved lengthwise (backbone removed)
Lemon wedges as a garnish

Combine the garlic, ginger, paprika, and cayenne in a small food processor. With processor running, add the lemon juice and olive oil in a steady stream to form a paste. Add the cilantro, and the onions. Add pepper to taste. Mix again. Rub chicken with paste and let stand for 2 hours at room temperature or overnight in the refrigerator.

Bring the chicken to room temperature. Grill it over medium high heat for 12 minutes on each side or until thigh juices run clear. Serve with lemon wedges.

Spanish-Style Turkey Cutlets

Serves 4

½ **cup honey**
½ **cup olive oil**
3 **tablespoons sherry vinegar or dry sherry**
2 **tablespoons cumin**
1 **tablespoon garlic, finely minced**
1 **teaspoon pepper**
4 **turkey cutlets, pounded**

Warm the honey until it liquefies. Add the olive oil, sherry, cumin, garlic, and pepper. Mix well and transfer to a glass dish. Add the turkey cutlets and marinate them overnight in the refrigerator.

Bring the cutlets to room temperature and grill them over medium high heat for 3 to 4 minutes on each side. The honey may darken the turkey during cooking, so baste the cutlets frequently and turn them often.

Grilled Chicken Breasts with Honey and Sesame

Serves 6

¾ **cup honey**
3 **tablespoons sesame oil**
1½ **teaspoons cinnamon**
1 **teaspoon cumin**
1 **tablespoon olive oil**
2 **tablespoons fresh lemon juice**
6 **chicken breasts, boneless and skinless**

Warm the honey until it liquefies. Add the sesame oil, spices, oil, and lemon. Place the chicken breasts in a glass dish and pour the marinade over them. Marinate the chicken at room temperature for 1 hour or overnight in the refrigerator.

Bring the chicken breasts to room temperature and reserve the marinade.

Grill the breasts over medium high heat for 5 minutes on each side. The honey in the marinade will cause the chicken to brown quickly, so turn the breasts frequently and baste them often with the reserved marinade.

Thai-Style Grilled Chicken Salad

Serves 2

3 tablespoons fish sauce
3 tablespoons fresh lime or lemon juice
2 tablespoons fresh mint, finely chopped
1 tablespoon honey
3½ teaspoons garlic, minced
1 teaspoon serrano chili with seeds, minced
½ cup olive oil
2 chicken breasts (approx 8 oz. each),
     skinless and boneless

Salad

1 teaspoon pepper
1 small head romaine lettuce, torn into
     bite-sized pieces

Garnish

1 yellow pepper, cut into matchstick strips
1 sweet red pepper, cut into matchstick strips
¼ cup chopped fresh mint
2 tablespoons reserved marinade
2 small tomatoes, cut into wedges

Combine the fish sauce, lime or lemon juice, mint, honey, garlic, chili, and olive oil in a shallow glass dish. Place the chicken in the mixture and marinate it in the refrigerator for 2 hours or overnight.

Reserve the marinade. Grill the chicken for 5 minutes on each side over medium high heat.

Slice the chicken and arrange on a salad made of romaine lettuce and pepper, tossed together.

Place the yellow and red peppers, the ¼ cup chopped mint, and the reserved marinade in a bowl. With your hands squeeze the peppers, mint, and marinade together to allow peppers to absorb flavor. Arrange the mixture around the chicken and garnish with the tomato wedges.

Chicken Fajitas

Serves 6

The great fajitas you get in Mexican restaurants and the ones we serve at the Dew Drop Inn are easy to prepare at home. Make your own guacamole, and set out plenty of salsa, sour cream, green onions, shredded lettuce, and shredded cheddar cheese. Warm up lots of flour tortillas on the grill. Sauté some onions and green peppers and throw a fajita party!

6   **chicken breasts**
6   **tablespoons of Dew Drop Inn Spice Rub (p. 33)**
1   **cup dry white wine**
⅓   **cup vegetable oil**
2   **tablespoons cilantro, chopped**
      Juice of 1 lime
½   **cup orange juice**

Place the chicken breasts between two sheets of wax paper and pound them into thin cutlets. Rub both sides generously with Dew Drop Inn Spice Rub.

Combine the wine, oil, cilantro, and juices in a shallow glass dish. Add the chicken and marinate it overnight in the refrigerator.

Bring the chicken to room temperature and grill it over medium high heat for 4 minutes on each side. Transfer it to a carving board, slice it into thin strips, and serve.

Grilled Tandoori Chicken

Serves 4

6   garlic cloves
1   piece ginger (approx. 1 in. long), peeled
1   cup plain yogurt
    Juice of 1 lemon
1   teaspoon salt
1   teaspoon cayenne
1   tablespoon paprika
1   teaspoon cumin
½   cup olive oil
1   chicken (approx. 3 lb.), cut into serving pieces
    Lemon wedges
    Thinly sliced onion

Using a food processor, with the motor running, drop in garlic cloves and ginger. Add the yogurt, lemon juice, salt, cayenne, paprika, and cumin and process to combine. Add the oil in steady stream. Pour the mixture over the chicken in a glass dish and marinate it overnight in the refrigerator, turning once or twice.

Bring the chicken to room temperature and grill it over medium high heat for 12 to 15 minutes on each side. Serve it with the lemon wedges and thinly sliced onion.

Indian Chicken

Serves 8

1	chicken (approx. 3 lb.), cut into 8 pieces
2	cups plain yogurt
2	teaspoon ground coriander
2	teaspoons paprika
1	teaspoon turmeric
	Juice of 1 lime
1	teaspoon honey
½	garlic clove, minced
1	2-inch piece ginger, peeled and grated

Pierce the chicken all over with a fork. Combine all of the remaining ingredients and spread half of the mixture over the chicken, rubbing it in well. Place the chicken and the rest of the mixture in a shallow glass dish or a zip-top plastic bag and marinate it, covered or closed, for at least 4 hours or overnight in the refrigerator.

Bring it to room temperature, reserving the marinade.

Place the chicken skin side down as high above the coals as possible, and grill it until it is lightly browned. Turn it over and cook the other side until it is lightly browned. Baste the chicken frequently with the reserved marinade. Lower the grill for the last 15 minutes and cook the chicken, turning and basting frequently, until it is brown and the skin is crisp. Serve any remaining marinade separately as a sauce.

Jerk Chicken Thighs

Serves 4

This is a mild version of Jamaican jerk spices, which usually include Scotch bonnet peppers. This is not as spicy as the Jamaican version, but it's just as good. Serve this dish with a salad and black beans and rice.

4   small fresh green or red chilies or pickled jalapeños
4   green onion, trimmed
2   tablespoons red wine vinegar
1   tablespoon oil
1   tablespoon ailspice
1   teaspoon salt
½   teaspoon pepper
½   teaspoon cinnamon
⅛   teaspoon nutmeg
8   boneless chicken thighs

In a small food processor chop the chilies and the green onions. If you chop the chilies by hand, wear rubber gloves to protect your hands. Add all of the remaining ingredients except the chicken and process the mixture until a paste forms.

In a shallow glass dish lay the boned chicken thighs flat and spread the chili paste over them. Marinate the chicken thighs for 2 hours or overnight in the refrigerator, turning once and spreading the paste over them.

Bring them to room temperature and grill them over medium high heat for 4 minutes on each side or until the juices run clear.

Spicy Grilled Citrus Turkey

Serves 6

1	can (6 oz.) frozen orange juice concentrate, thawed
½	cup canned tomato puree
¼	cup honey
1	teaspoon minced orange zest
1	teaspoon minced lemon zest
1	teaspoon minced lime zest
3	tablespoons fresh lemon juice
3	tablespoons fresh lime juice
4	garlic cloves, pressed
1	teaspoon dried thyme
¾	teaspoon cayenne
¾	teaspoon pepper
1	teaspoon salt
6	turkey cutlets

Combine the orange juice, tomato puree, honey, orange, lemon, and lime zest, lemon, and lime juice, garlic, thyme, cayenne, pepper, and salt in a shallow glass dish. Add the cutlets and marinate them for 2 hours or overnight in the refrigerator.

Bring the cutlets to room temperature and grill them over medium high heat for 4 to 5 minutes on each side.

Chicken Teriyaki

Serves 4

Garnish this simple dish with orange slices and serve it with Cold Sesame Noodles (page 147).

¾ **cup chopped, peeled fresh ginger**
2   **tablespoons garlic, minced**
½ **cup sugar**
1   **cup sake**
½ **cup soy sauce**
4   **chicken breasts, boneless and skinless, pounded flat**

Combine the ginger, garlic, sugar, sake, and soy sauce in a shallow glass dish. Add the chicken and marinate it for 2 hours or overnight in the refrigerator.

Bring the chicken breasts to room temperature and grill them over medium high heat for 5 minutes on each side or until the juices run clear.

◇ 7 ◇

Great Vegetables and Accompaniment Salads

Grilled Teriyaki Eggplant

Serves 4–6 as a side dish

2   large eggplants, cut into ½-inch slices
2   cups Teriyaki Marinade (page 26)

Place the eggplant slices in a glass dish and pour the marinade over them. Marinate at room temperature for 1 hour. Grill the eggplant over medium high heat for 5 minutes on each side.

Grilled Caponata

Yields 6–8 cups

Caponata means "relish" in Italian and many good Italian cooks have their own version of it. Grilling gives the eggplant a smoky flavor, and cocoa powder is my secret ingredient. This is perfect as a snack or as a light vegetarian supper with mozzarella cheese and fresh garden tomatoes. Add your own special secret ingredients such as fresh basil or oregano.

1	medium eggplant (approx. 3 lb.), cut into ⅝-inch-thick slices
2	large red onions (approx. 2 lb.), peeled and sliced into five ½-inch-thick slices
⅓	cup virgin olive oil
2	teaspoons sifted unsweetened cocoa powder
¾	cup chopped canned whole tomatoes
1	tablespoon capers
8	green olives, pitted and sliced
8	kalamata olives, pitted and quartered
¼	cup balsamic vinegar
	Salt and pepper to taste

Brush the eggplant and onion slices with the olive oil and grill them for 4 minutes on each side or until the eggplant is well browned and soft and the onion is slightly brown but not soft. Set aside to cool.

Coarsely chop the onion and eggplant and transfer to a medium-sized bowl. Add the cocoa powder, tomatoes, capers, olive, and vinegar. Allow to sit at room temperature for an hour or two. Taste and adjust seasonings, adding salt and pepper to taste.

Grilled-Garlic Puree

Yields ½–¾ cup

Make a big batch of grilled garlic. Grilling garlic makes it sweet and delicious. Spread the pureed garlic on bread and grill it for instant garlic bread without butter. Use the puree in garlic vinaigrette to serve with grilled vegetables, or toss it into pasta and grilled vegetables for a quick pasta dinner. You can also serve this puree with roasted peppers and mozzarella cheese. Once you have this staple on hand, the possibilities are endless. The garlic puree will keep in the refrigerator for up to 2 weeks.

6   large whole garlic heads
3   sprigs fresh thyme, chopped or dried thyme
    Olive oil

With a sharp knife slice off the top of each head of garlic to expose the inner cloves. Place the garlic on a square of aluminum foil. Drizzle some olive oil and either place ½ a sprig of fresh thyme or sprinkle a couple pinches of dried thyme on them. Place the garlic heads on the grill. Grill them for 30 to 45 minutes. Allow them to cool.

Squeeze the garlic cloves out of their skin and mash them with a fork. Place the puree in a small plastic container and cover it with a thin layer of the remaining olive oil. Refrigerate the puree and use as needed.

Grilled Plantains and Chayote

Serves 4 as a side dish

These Latin American vegetables serve as an excellent accompaniment to Jerk Chicken Thighs. Plantains are not as sweet as bananas and are more fibrous, so they grill up nicely.

2   **plantains or**
1   **chayote, sliced**
1   **teaspoon olive oil**
    Chili powder
    Fresh cilantro, chopped
2   **limes, quartered**

Brush the vegetables with the olive oil and grill them over medium high heat for 3 to 4 minutes on each side. Dust them with chili powder, sprinkle them with chopped cilantro, and squeeze fresh lime juice over them.

Gingery Pineapple–Red Pepper Kebabs

Serves 4 as a side dish

Cook up any of the soy-based marinade fish recipes; these kebabs are a great accompaniment to them. If you can't find preserved ginger in your supermarket, use minced fresh ginger.

¼ cup melted butter or margarine
8 small pieces preserved ginger
¼ cup dry white wine
1 large ripe pineapple, cored, peeled, and cut into 1½-inch chunks
1 large red bell pepper, seeded and quartered
1 large green bell pepper, seeded and quartered

In a small saucepan combine the butter, ginger and wine. Warm the mixture for a few minutes to release the flavor of the ginger.

Thread the pineapple and pepper chunks onto the skewers. Brush them with the ginger-flavored sauce.

Grill the kebabs over medium high heat for 4 minutes on each side. Brush them frequently with the sauce.

Grilled Ratatouille Sandwich

Serves 4

This sandwich is perfect for picnics. Make it early in the day or grill the vegetables the night before. Assemble the sandwich and wrap it in foil. This sandwich only improves in flavor and needs no refrigeration.

5	garlic cloves, peeled and chopped
¾	cup olive oil
2	sprigs fresh rosemary, chopped
3	medium zucchini, trimmed and cut lengthwise
1	large green bell pepper, seeded and quartered
2	small eggplants (approx. ¾ lb. each), peeled and cut into ¾-inch-thick slices
1	large red bell pepper, seeded and quartered
1	large red onion, peeled and cut into ½-inch-thick slices
3	large ripe tomatoes, cut into 1-inch-thick slices
15	Niçoise olives, pitted and coarsely chopped
4	anchovy fillets, rinsed, dried, and finely chopped
1	long sourdough baguette, sliced lengthwise
	Salt and pepper to taste

Combine the garlic, oil, and rosemary. Brush all of the vegetables with oil mixture and grill them over medium high heat until tender. The peppers and onions will take a few minutes longer than the eggplant and zucchini. Add the tomatoes last and cook them for only 1 or 2 minutes on each side.

Brush the cut sides of the baguette with the oil and garlic mixture and grill the bread for 1 or 2 minutes on each side.

Layer the grilled vegetables down the length of one side of the bread. Sprinkle with the olives and the anchovy fillets, and season with salt and pepper. Cover with other side of bread. Wrap sandwich tightly in foil and allow flavors to blend for 1 to 2 hours. Slice into fourths and serve.

Grilled-Tomato Vinaigrette

Yields 3 cups

This sauce should be served fresh. Therefore, be sure to prepare it on the day you plan to use it. Also, do not reheat it when pouring it over your favorite pasta or grilled fish. Serve it at room temperature.

8–9 medium plum tomatoes
½ cup extra virgin olive oil
¼ cup mixed chopped fresh herbs, such as basil, marjoram, tarragon, thyme, or fennel
¼ cup fresh lemon juice
2 large garlic cloves, crushed

Rub the tomatoes with a small amount of the olive oil and grill them over dying coals or over medium heat for 3 minutes on each side, or until the skin bursts a little and blackens slightly. Set them aside until they are cool enough to handle. Remove the skins of the tomatoes. Coarsely chop the cool tomatoes. Using your hands, remove them from the cutting surface, leaving the seeds and juices behind. Transfer the tomato chunks to a medium-size glass or porcelain bowl. Add the chopped herbs, the lemon juice, garlic, and the remaining oil. Let the mixture sit for 2 or 3 hours at room temperature. Remove the crushed garlic cloves before serving.

Grilled Polenta

Serves 4 as a side dish

Polenta is the Italian version of cornmeal mush. My mother used to fry it and serve it for breakfast with maple syrup. In today's healthy cooking, we grill it.

1	cup cornmeal
3	cups water
1	teaspoon salt
1	cup frozen whole-kernel corn
¼	red bell pepper, minced
2	tablespoons sour cream or low-fat yogurt
	Several dashes of Worcestershire sauce
	Several dashes of hot pepper sauce

Mix the cornmeal and water in a medium saucepan and cook it over medium heat for 10 to 15 minutes, stirring frequently. Add the salt, corn, red pepper, sour cream or yogurt, Worcestershire sauce, and hot pepper sauce. Cook for an additional 5 minutes, stirring constantly. Transfer the mixture to a loaf pan or a 9X9X3-inch glass baking dish. Allow to set overnight in the refrigerator.

Cut the polenta loaf into ½-inch slices and brush the slices with your favorite basting sauce. Grill them over medium high heat, basting often, until heated through, about 5 minutes on each side.

Roasted Peppers

Roasting peppers is simple, and the results are delicious! Use a combination of green, red, and yellow peppers. Roast a bunch at a time, and use them throughout the week in pasta salads and grilled caponata, or add them to your favorite potato salad. Serve these peppers with mozzarella, sliced tomatoes, good Italian bread, and a green salad for a light and satisfying summertime dinner. Cover the roasted peppers with olive oil and store them in the refrigerator in a covered plastic container. They will keep for several weeks. They can also be kept at room temperature for several hours.

6   bell peppers
¼   cup extra virgin olive oil

Brush the peppers with some of the olive oil. Place them on a grill over high heat. Allow each side to blacken, turning with tongs and taking care not to pierce the skin.

Place the roasted peppers in a large paper bag. Place that bag inside a sealed plastic bag. Allow peppers to steam for at least 15 minutes or for as long as an hour. Remove the peppers from the bag and carefully peel them, using a knife for any stubborn spots. Slice into the natural triangle at the top of the pepper. Run under water to remove seeds. Arrange the pepper on a platter. Drizzle the remaining olive oil over them.

Grilled Vegetables with
Roasted-Garlic Vinaigrette

Serves 6–8 as a side dish

Serve these vegetables with sliced tomatoes and a loaf of good Italian bread for a light summer supper or lunch.

3	large eggplants, cut diagonally into ½-inch slices
3	large zucchini, cut diagonally into ½-inch slices
1	large red bell pepper, seeded and cut into 3-inch chunks
6	large shiitake mushrooms
	Olive oil for grilling
	Assorted greens such as watercress, red leaf lettuce, and arugula
½	cup fresh basil, shredded
2	tablespoons Grilled-Garlic Puree (page 131)
1½	tablespoons balsamic vinegar
⅓	cup olive oil

Brush the vegetables with olive oil and place them in an oiled hinged grilling basket. Grill them over medium heat for 4 to 5 minutes per side or until tender.

Toss together the assorted greens and basil.

Mix together the garlic puree, vinegar, and olive oil.

Arrange the assorted greens on a platter. Place the vegetables on top. Drizzle the roasted-garlic vinaigrette over the vegetables and assorted greens.

Grilled Green Tomatoes

Serves 4

What to do with the last of the green tomatoes from your garden? Grill them!

4 green tomatoes, cut in ½-inch slices
   Cajun-Style Spice Rub (p. 35)
   Olive oil

Brush the tomato slices with olive oil and dust them with the spice rub. Grill them over medium high heat for 3 to 4 minutes on each side.

Grilled Corn on the Cob

Serves 6

6   ears of fresh-picked corn
¼   cup corn oil
½   teaspoon chili powder (optional)

Partially shuck the corn, leaving just enough husks to cover the corn. Remove the silk. Brush the ears with corn oil. Wrap them in aluminum foil and grill them over medium high heat for 3 to 4 minutes on each side. Remove them from the heat and carefully unwrap them, twisting off the husk. Dust them with chili powder if desired.

Grilled Potato Wedges

Serves 4

Here are two versions of grilled potato wedges. Using the same basic principle, you can make your own version, using your favorite spice rub and oil.

4   large raw potatoes scrubbed but not peeled
½   cup melted butter
¼   teaspoon paprika
¼   teaspoon garlic salt
⅛   teaspoon pepper

Parboil the potatoes for 10 minutes. Quarter them lengthwise. Combine the butter, paprika, garlic salt, and pepper, and brush the mixture on the potatoes. Grill the potatoes for 15 minutes, basting frequently with remaining butter.

Herbed Potato Wedges

4   large potatoes, scrubbed but not peeled
½   cup melted butter
2   tablespoons fresh parsley and thyme, chopped
    Salt and pepper to taste

Parboil the potatoes for 10 minutes. Quarter them lengthwise. Combine the butter, herbs, salt, and pepper. Brush the mixture on the potatoes. Grill the potatoes for 15 minutes, basting frequently with remaining butter.

Grilled Potato Salad

Serves 6–8 as a side dish

2   **lbs. large white potatoes, cut into ¼-inch slices**
    Olive oil for grilling
¼ **cup green onions, chopped**
¼ **cup fresh dill, chopped**
½ **cup celery, chopped**
1   **teaspoon paprika**
1   **teaspoon dry mustard**
    Pepper to taste
½ **cup plain low-fat yogurt**
½ **cup low-fat mayonnaise**

Brush the potato slices lightly with olive oil. Grill them over medium high heat in an oiled grilling basket for 4 minutes on each side or until they are tender. Remove from heat and let cool.

Place the potatoes in a large bowl and add the green onions, dill, celery, paprika, and mustard. Add pepper to taste. Toss well. In a small bowl mix the yogurt and mayonnaise. Add small amounts of the yogurt mixture to the potato salad, stirring, until you get the desired consistency.

Grilled-Vegetable Hummus

Serves 8 as an appetizer

This recipe is only a guide. You may use any combination of leftover grilled vegetables. Serve the hummus as an appetizer with grilled pita, black olives, and canned stuffed grape leaves. You can buy tahini (sesame seed paste) in any Asian market.

4	grilled zucchini
4	grilled yellow squash
4	grilled red bell peppers
1	grilled red onion
2	tablespoons garlic, chopped
	Juice of 3 lemons
1	cup olive oil
2	tablespoons salt
⅛	tablespoons cayenne
1	cup tahini
2	tablespoons cumin

Puree the vegetables in a food processor. Add all of the remaining ingredients and mix well. Adjust the seasonings. Flavor will grow stronger overnight in the refrigerator.

Coleslaw

Serves 6–8 as a side dish

½   **medium green cabbage, finely shredded**
1   **small onion, thinly sliced**
½   **cup sour gherkins or other pickles, thinly sliced**
1   **garlic clove, minced**
⅓   **cup mayonnaise**
2   **tablespoons white wine vinegar**
    Salt and pepper to taste

Combine all the ingredients. Season with salt and pepper. Refrigerate for several hours before serving.

Cold Sesame Noodles

Serves 6–8 as a side dish

Everyone loves the cold sesame noodles served in Chinese restaurants. They are easy to prepare, and they make a great accompaniment to simple grilled fish or chicken.

1	**pound uncooked linguini or spaghetti**
4	**tablespoons sesame oil**
¼	**cup crunchy peanut butter**
⅛	**cup honey**
1	**tablespoon red wine vinegar**
1	**tablespoon ginger, minced**
1	**tablespoon garlic**
¾	**tablespoon hot pepper sauce**
1	**tablespoon soy sauce**
½	**cup vegetable oil**
	Salt and pepper to taste
¼	**cup green onions, thinly sliced**
½	**cucumber, peeled, seeded, and thinly sliced**

In boiling salted water, cook the pasta al dente. Drain it and rinse it well under cold running water. Toss it lightly with about 1 tablespoon of the sesame oil. Set aside.

In a separate bowl, mix the peanut butter, honey, vinegar, ginger, garlic, hot pepper sauce, and soy sauce. Gradually whip in the remaining sesame oil and the vegetable oil in a thin stream. Season with salt and pepper. Pour the dressing over the pasta and toss well. Garnish with chopped green onions and cucumber.

Black Bean and Corn Salad

Serves 4–6 as a side dish

This is a great picnic salad.

2 cans black beans (16 oz. each), drained
2 packages (10 oz. each) frozen, whole-kernel corn, thawed and drained
1 pint cherry tomatoes, quartered
1 medium red onion, finely chopped
½ cup fresh cilantro, chopped
½ cup fresh parsley, chopped
1 tablespoon chili powder
2 tablespoons pickled jalapeño, chopped
¼ cup olive oil
3 tablespoons lime juice
   Salt and pepper to taste

Mix all of the ingredients in a medium bowl. Season with salt and pepper.

My Baked Beans

Serves 6–8 as a side dish

I love great slow-cooked baked beans, but I never seem to have the time to cook them. I sometimes use bacon in my beans, but this healthy version is just as good. Top with bread crumbs and season with Cajun-Style Spice rub, if desired.

2   garlic cloves, chopped
2   large yellow onions, chopped
2   tablespoons vegetable oil
2   cans (30 oz. each) vegetarian baked beans
¼   cup molasses
¼   cup maple syrup
½   cup brown sugar
½   cup ketchup
2   tablespoons dry mustard

Sauté the garlic and onions in the vegetable oil in a small skillet over medium low heat until soft. Combine the garlic, onion, beans, molasses, maple syrup, brown sugar, ketchup, and mustard in a glass baking dish. Bake at 350° F. for 45 minutes.

Tabbouleh Salad

Serves 6 to 8

Bulgur has been around for a long time, but now it's a hot grain. Also known as cracked wheat, it is filled with vitamins and wholesome goodness. It also has a great nutty flavor. This salad is refreshing for summertime, and it keeps well for picnics. It is the perfect accompaniment to many of the grilled fish and chicken recipes containing coriander and cumin.

1	**cup bulgur**
1	**cup cold water**
½	**cup fresh lemon juice**
⅔	**cup olive oil**
1	**cup fresh mint, coarsely chopped**
1	**cup Italian parsley, coarsely chopped**
½	**cup red onion, finely chopped**
2	**teaspoons garlic, minced**
1	**teaspoon salt**
4	**ripe tomatoes**
1	**large cucumber, peeled, seeded, and cut diced**
	Fresh mint for garnish

Combine the bulgur, water, lemon juice, and ⅓ cup of the olive oil in a large bowl. Mix well and let stand for 30 minutes at room temperature.

Fluff the bulgur mixture with a fork. Add the mint, parsley, red onion, garlic, salt, and remaining olive oil. Toss well with a fork.

Add the tomatoes and cucumber and toss again. Adjust the seasonings and let the salad stand at room temperature for 30 minutes.

Garnish with fresh mint.